Outdoor Kitchens

ideas for planning, designing, and entertaining

Outdoor Kitchens

ideas for planning, designing, and entertaining

JOSEPH R. PROVEY
OWEN LOCKWOOD

CREATIVE HOMEOWNER®, Upper Saddle River, New Jersey

Outdoor Kitchens
Produced by Home & Garden Editorial Services
Authors: Joseph R. Provey, Owen Lockwood
Contributors: Roy Barnhart, MaryAnn Kopp
Layout: Jill Potvin Schoff, Venera Alexandrova
Copy Editor: Owen Lockwood
Editorial Assistant: MaryAnn Kopp
Photo Prepress: Carl Weese
Illustrations: Bob La Pointe
Front Cover Photography: courtesy of Western Red
    Cedar Lumber Association
Inside Front Cover Photography: *(top)* courtesy of Heat & Glo;
    (bottom) courtesy of McHale Landscape Design, Inc.,
    photography by Erin Brooke Bogan
Back Cover Photography: *(top)* courtesy of Fogazzo Wood
    Fired Ovens & Barbecues; *(bottom right)* courtesy of
    KitchenAid; *(bottom left)* Crandall & Crandall
Inside Back Cover Photography: *(top)* courtesy of Cal Spas;
    (bottom) courtesy of Progress Lighting

Creative Homeowner
VP, Publisher: Timothy O. Bakke
Production Director: Kimberly H. Vivas
Art Director: David Geer
Managing Editor: Fran Donegan
Senior Editor: Kathie Robitz
Editorial Assistants: Jennifer Calvert and Nora Grace

Current Printing (last digit)
10 9 8 7 6 5 4 3 2 1

Outdoor Kitchens, First Edition
Library of Congress Control Number: 2006397267
ISBN-10: 1-58011-349-4
ISBN-13: 978-1-58011-349-6

CREATIVE HOMEOWNER®
A Division of Federal Marketing Corp.
24 Park Way
Upper Saddle River, NJ 07458
www.creativehomeowner.com

ACKNOWLEDGMENTS

We would like to thank the many architects, photographers, and outdoor-kitchen product manufacturers who made this book possible, including designer/photographer Lars Dalsgaard, Sergio de Paula of Fogazzo Wood Fired Ovens and Barbecues, Chicago Specialty Gardens, stylist/photographer Sudi Scull, McHale Landscape Design, Stecks Nursery and Landscaping, Chuck and Barbara Crandall of Crandall & Crandall Photography, Pete Bleyer of Pete Bleyer Studio, and the Western Red Cedar Lumber Association.

CONTENTS

Why Build an Outdoor Kitchen?

REDISCOVER
THE
OUTDOORS

Because many people find themselves living in a digital world of cell phones, laptops, PDAs, and e-mail for a dozen or more hours each day, the allure of cooking and dining outdoors is not surprising. It's a way to feel connected to the great outdoors without having to jump on a jet or pull out into traffic to get there. It also reminds many of us of simpler days: camping trips, perhaps, or family picnics and barbecues. "Making do," without relying on the gadgetry of an indoor kitchen, assures us that our survival skills have not been completely lost. In addition, being outdoors creates a sense of romance and adventure. Fire, wind, the sun and stars, flora, and fauna were the only entertainment mankind had for millennia—and are still more compelling than what you'll find on TV.

Of course, few of us have the time and inclination to cook and eat outside in the manner of our ancestors—building fires from scratch to boil water and roast hunks of meat. This is why today's outdoor kitchens make sense. They allow you to prepare and serve a great meal and still have time to catch a movie, help the kids with their homework, take an art class, or simply kick back with friends and family.

There are additional practical reasons to install an outdoor kitchen and

Build a full-featured outdoor kitchen, such as this porch-covered design, or keep costs down by sticking to the basics: a sink, grill, counter, and cooler.

dining area as well. If your house is small but you like to entertain big groups, outdoor kitchens and dining areas are a great way to do it. The average dining room feels crowded with six or eight people, but your deck or patio won't. If you live in a warm climate, outdoor kitchens are also a good way to keep the heat out of the house. Many include sinks and running water to facilitate cleanup. With a roof, an outdoor kitchen lets you cook outdoors even when it's raining. Finally, most people will agree that food is more flavorful when eaten outside.

What Is an Outdoor Kitchen?

Definitions vary, but most agree that an outdoor kitchen includes at least one cooking appliance, a food-preparation surface, and storage. Stricter definitions add a sink with running water and refrigeration. As such, they are still relatively new to most of the country. In fact, just a decade ago it was difficult to find examples outside the Southwest. That has changed. Today there are more than one million full-fledged outdoor kitchens nationwide, and the hottest growth markets are where you would least expect: the Midwest and Northeast.

A refrigerator makes outdoor meal prep as easy and efficient as indoor cooking. The unit left of the grill above is large enough to hold drinks, marinades, sauces, and condiments.

Vessel sinks, left, look great outdoors and are great for washing fruits and veggies. If you're planning to wash dinnerware outside, however, you'll want something more practical. See Chapter 7.

Unfortunately, unless you live in the Southwest, local designers and contractors probably will not have much experience with building outdoor kitchens. In addition, the designs from that region may not be suitable for other parts of the country. This is how *Outdoor Kitchens* can help. In Part 1, "Get Started," you'll explore every facet of designing and building an outdoor kitchen: deciding where to put it, choosing a layout, determining a budget, and selecting a flooring material. You'll also learn how to improve comfort, ensure safety, and set up the perfect dining area.

Part 2, "Outfit Your Kitchen," offers in-depth guidance on cabinetry, countertops, faucets and sinks, refrigerators, grills, and a variety of other cooking appliances. There is plenty of information on other amenities as well, including outdoor lighting, outdoor sound systems, and even decorations such as outdoor carpeting, plants, and planters. Although some of the more extreme amenities (weatherproof TV, anyone?) are here for readers who want to know all of the options, the focus is on good design, good value, and common sense.

Part 3, "Design Gallery," presents an assortment of professionally designed outdoor kitchens. A moderately skilled homeowner can build some of them for less than $1,500. Others require professional help and a bigger investment. In either case, you will find many ideas to incorporate in your outdoor kitchen.

A wide range of flooring choices, above, for outdoor kitchens and dining areas is available to you.

An outdoor kitchen with a roof, below, can be built with indoor luxuries, such as a TV, stereo, and lighting.

PART 1: GET STARTED

CHAPTER 1

Where to Put Your Outdoor Kitchen

CHOOSING THE RIGHT SITE

W here to build your outdoor kitchen may seem very obvious to you. Nevertheless, take a few moments to examine all suitable sites. Walk around your property and take note of locations that feel good to you. If a possible site is high off the ground, bring along a stepladder so you can view the site from the level at which you would be cooking and dining. Revisit candidate sites at the time of day you'd likely be using them and check for things like sun and shade, whether the neighbors can see the outdoor kitchen (should that matter to you), and the direction of prevailing winds. Try to anticipate how all of these variables will change with the seasons. Also consider your options for any electrical, water, or gas hookups that you may need.

If you're thinking about building an outdoor kitchen on an existing patio or deck, you already know the space pretty well. But is it big enough to accommodate the grill and appliances you hope to install? Will additional footings need to be dug to support the grill island of your dreams? And is it really the best location? There's no sense in investing hundreds or thousands of dollars in a spot where you're not going to be happy. You may want to discuss some of your options with a landscape architect.

If you choose a location far from the house, such as this pool-side kitchen, you'll likely want to include a sink, refrigerator, and plenty of storage.

A grill counter under trees, above, offers respite from the sun and wind, but it's likely to mean some extra cleanup.

Near or Far?

There is an even more fundamental question to consider before choosing a site for an outdoor kitchen: should you build it as close as possible to your indoor kitchen, or well away from the house near a yard attraction, such as a garden or pool? There can be good reasons for each choice, and your decision will largely affect many of the design decisions that follow, not to mention the cost of the project.

The closer you build your outdoor kitchen to your indoor kitchen, the simpler it can be. After all, carrying a tray laden with dishes, napkins, and utensils a dozen or so steps is no big deal. Running back inside for the frozen dessert at the end of the meal is no big deal either. Being close to the indoor kitchen will also allow you to prepare parts of meals that require the finesse and control of your cooktop. It also makes it a lot easier when you want to cook outdoors but eat indoors. Just as important, guests will have convenient access to your home's bathrooms.

There are other big benefits as well. The biggest is what you build upon. Chances are you already have a deck or patio that

A site under deep eaves, opposite, offers protection but requires a range hood to avoid a smoky dining area.

can be used as the foundation of your outdoor kitchen. If not, it's likely that the yard near your back door is flat and ready to be built upon. In addition, it will be far easier and less costly to hook up to utilities such as water, gas, and electricity if you select a site that's close to the house. Winterizing water lines will be less complicated as well.

Smart Tip — Dock the Barge

Try to avoid plunking your outdoor kitchen in the middle of your backyard, where it's likely to look like a barge that's broken its moorings and will get in the way of other yard activities. The best sites for outdoor kitchens are often partially enclosed. Porches, for example, offer some obvious benefits. The lee of a tall wall that surrounds the yard is another traditional site. House and outbuilding walls, fences, and areas protected by the natural terrain all offer opportunities.

Remote Outdoor Kitchens

On the other hand, a remote kitchen and dining area may take better advantage of a view, beautiful backyard landscaping, or the ideal exposure to sun and wind. Remote locations often allow greater privacy and can enhance the enjoyment of recreational home features, such as a pool or tennis court. And if it's the feeling of camping out you seek, outdoor dining and cooking areas that are at your back door just don't cut it.

Remote outdoor kitchens are more likely to be full featured, with built-in grills, multiple burners, a fridge, counter space, and lots of storage. You're far more likely to have to build a detached deck or a patio—and run electrical, water, and gas lines. And a roof is often desirable to keep surfaces from becoming messy due to tree and bird droppings.

But such a kitchen really does feel like a getaway…and keeps most of the mess well away from the house. This would be especially important if you plan to do some real barbecuing, using a smoker, for instance. The trade-off, of course, is the hefty price tag that comes with such a space. And where do you stop? Once you have duplicated your cooking and dining capability in the back corner of your property, can a cottage with an outdoor bathroom and bedroom be far behind?

Remote kitchens, however, do not have to be elaborate or expensive. You just need to be resourceful. Yes, you will need to build a level, firm surface, but consider ice chests in place of refrigerators, a freestanding grill instead of one that is built-in, and a countertop and hose-fed sink on a cart in place of permanent cabinets. To shelter your dinner guests, there are plenty of modestly priced tents and gazebos made with screens or durable outdoor fabric. The frames are corrosion resistant and many feature washable coverings that can be removed during the winter and replaced if necessary. Add a fire pit and gas or candle lanterns for light, heat, and ambience.

When viewed from the house, left, this outdoor kitchen is a focal point in the landscape. Up close, above, it offers shade and sustenance.

Smart Tip Before You Dig

Check out the location of everything on your property that is near the planned construction site. Chances are, a deck or patio will limit access to, or interfere with, at least one of them. It's common, for example, to have exterior spigots end up below deck level. You can either relocate them or build a small trapdoor for access. Also, do not plan to build a deck or concrete patio over or even near a septic tank. Setbacks of 15 to 20 feet are usually required. Other in-ground obstacles may include buried well-water piping, electrical lines to the garage or pool, existing gas lines to the barbecue, sump pump and rainwater drains, basement doors, and buried oil tanks.

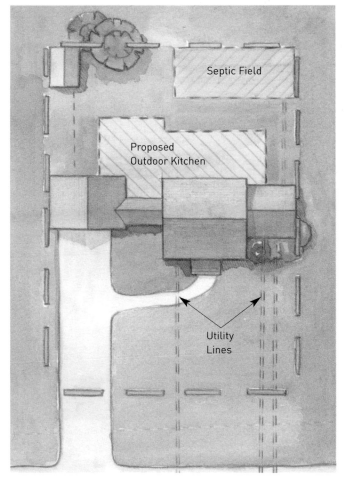

Septic Field

Proposed Outdoor Kitchen

Utility Lines

Under the yard there is more going on than most of us think. Be sure to check before you dig.

Get the Exposure Right

If you forget to consider exposure to the sun when choosing a site for your outdoor kitchen, you may end up broiling sooner than the burgers. Assuming you have more than one option for where to build your kitchen, exposure to the sun may be the deciding factor. Sun exposure is determined by a candidate site's orientation to the sun's daily path. A south-facing outdoor kitchen, even if built close to the house, will receive sun almost all day. Outdoor kitchens built on east- and west-facing decks or patios get sun in the morning and afternoon, respectively. Southeast- or southwest-facing kitchens will receive the sun for longer periods than those that face due east or west. North-facing sites, unless you extend them beyond the shadow of your house, will receive little or no sun for much of the day.

To decide what's best for you, think about when you are most likely to be doing your outdoor cooking and dining. If it's for morning breakfasts and brunches, southeast- or east-facing may be acceptable. Afternoon and evening users would probably prefer a southwest- or west-facing deck. If you live in a climate where summers are cool, perhaps south-facing is the ideal orientation. Conversely, if you live where it's warm most of the time, a shaded northern exposure may suit you.

Of course, you will need to take into account the shade thrown by nearby trees, walls, and buildings. Keep in mind that you can always create shade by planting trees or adding an overhead shade structure, such as a pergola or gazebo.

A southern exposure, right, helps keep mold and mildew at bay. Deep eaves and a large tree cool the cook on a hot day.

Pick the Perfect Sun Exposure

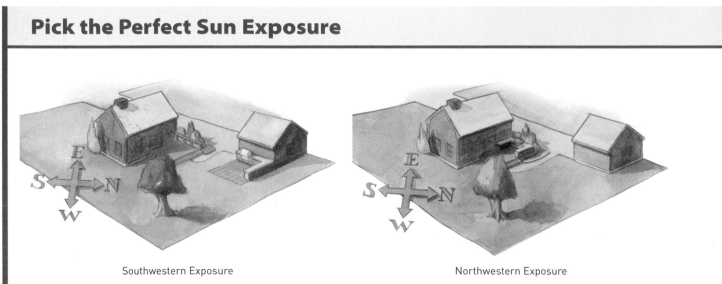

Southwestern Exposure

Northwestern Exposure

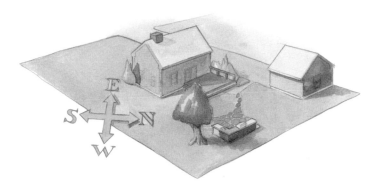

Northeastern Exposure

A southwestern exposure, far left, allows this outdoor kitchen to dry quickly after a rain. The shed offers protection from northeasterly winds.

A northwestern exposure, center, means this kitchen next to the house gets sun most of the afternoon and evening, the time when most people use an outdoor kitchen.

A northeastern exposure, near left, helps keep the afternoon crowd cool in the summer and lets the sun through once the leaves fall in autumn in this outdoor kitchen situated near a tree.

Wind Control

In many locations, wind is another factor to consider. If you live in a cool climate where the prevailing wind is frequently gusty, opt for the protected side of your house to increase the time you can enjoy your outdoor kitchen. Take advantage of natural windbreaks whenever possible. If neither works for your situation, you can build a windscreen or plant a windbreak. (See the illustration below.) If you live in a hot climate, the breeze may bring welcome relief from the heat. Prevailing winds are also a factor when it comes to placing cooking appliances, fire pits, and fireplaces because they will affect where the smoke drifts while cooking.

The lee of a house, garage, barn, or other structure provides shelter from the wind. The massive fireplace, right, performs the same function.

The Value of a Windbreak

A windbreak, typically a row of dense trees planted perpendicular to the prevailing wind, can greatly improve the comfort level of your outdoor culinary experience. The general rule is that a windbreak is effective for a distance of 30 times its height. For example, a 20-ft.-high row of conifers will reduce winds for a distance of about 600 ft.

If you live in an area where winds blow regularly, opt for a partially enclosed kitchen and dining area, such as the one above.

If storms howl, simply batten down the hatches, left, and make wind a nonfactor.

When You Can't Decide

A portable outdoor kitchen may be the answer if you can't decide where to build. It's also a good solution if you want to be able to take advantage of several good sites around your yard. For example, you may prefer a spot by the pool in the summer but want to be on your deck in the fall. There are many commercially available mobile-kitchen components from which to choose, including bars, refrigerators, and rolling cabinets with handy work surfaces.

A serving cart, right, can be wheeled wherever you need it most.

With all but the fridge on casters, this kitchen, below, can be rearranged as the sun moves and winds change.

Build a Kitchen Cart

Materials for the rolling kitchen cart shown here cost far less than a ready-made commercial cart. It includes a sink and can be used in conjunction with a portable grill to allow cooking anywhere in your yard. Roll it out when you need it, and roll it out of the way when you don't. Protect it from the elements with a large grill cover or tarp.

In addition to a sizable work surface, this unit features hooks for hanging utensils, ample shelving for cookware and table service, and heavy-duty casters for portability. The hose-fed sink can drain into a garden, gravel pit, or container. (See instructions for building the cart on page 26.)

An outdoor kitchen counter, with a sink, a burner, and storage, and accompanied by a portable grill, is an inexpensive but serviceable outdoor kitchen. Large casters or wheels allow you to use it in several locations.

An optional gas burner, placed on tiles to prevent countertop scorching, allows you to handle stove-top cooking tasks.

Build a Kitchen Cart (continued)

Kitchen Cart Materials

A: 2 pcs. $1\frac{1}{2}$ x $3\frac{1}{2}$ x $42\frac{3}{4}$ in. pine or fir
B: 2 pcs. $1\frac{1}{2}$ x $3\frac{1}{2}$ x $27\frac{1}{2}$ in. pine or fir
C: 1 pc. $1\frac{1}{2}$ x $1\frac{1}{2}$ x 62 in. pine or fir
D: 1 pc. $\frac{3}{4}$ x $5\frac{1}{2}$ x 65 in.
E: 1 pc. $\frac{3}{4}$ x $3\frac{1}{2}$ x $63\frac{1}{2}$ in.
F: 1 pc. $\frac{3}{4}$ x $3\frac{1}{2}$ x 62 in.
G: 2 pcs. $\frac{3}{4}$ x $3\frac{1}{2}$ x $60\frac{1}{2}$ in.
H: 2 pcs. $\frac{3}{4}$ x $3\frac{1}{2}$ x $25\frac{3}{4}$ in.
J: 2 pcs. $\frac{3}{4}$ x $3\frac{1}{2}$ x $22\frac{3}{4}$ in.
K: 16 pcs. $\frac{3}{4}$ x $3\frac{1}{2}$ x $22\frac{3}{4}$ in.
L: 12 pcs. $\frac{1}{2}$ x $1\frac{1}{2}$ x 25 in.**
M: 4 pcs. $\frac{1}{2}$ x $1\frac{1}{2}$ x 16 in.*
N: 2 pcs. $\frac{3}{4}$ x $\frac{3}{4}$ x $62\frac{7}{8}$ in.
O: 1 pc. $\frac{1}{2}$ x $\frac{1}{2}$ x $57\frac{3}{8}$ in.

Miscellaneous: butcher block (or other) counter-top ($1\frac{1}{2}$ x 25 x $64\frac{1}{2}$ in.) with 1-in. angle brackets (4); No. 6 screws ($1\frac{1}{8}$, $1\frac{1}{2}$, 2, $2\frac{1}{2}$ in.); No. 8 screws ($3\frac{1}{2}$ in.); casters with 4-in.-dia. wheels (2); locking casters with 4-in.-dia. wheels (2); bar with S-hooks and mounting brackets (1); exterior wood glue; primer; paint; varnish; bar sink; misc. water and drain fittings and connectors

* Long-point measurements (45-deg. cuts on ends)

** Long-point measurements (45-deg. cuts on ends); 2 pcs. require additional cutting

Create a shopping list using the cutting list above Buy your sink first, in case you need to modify counter-top dimensions to suit it.

1 **Taper legs B** using a table saw. Use one of the legs as a template to taper the lower half of legs A. Assemble the front and back frames by attaching rails E, F, and G as shown in the illustration on the previous page. Use water-resistant glue and screws to assemble.

3 **Nail the lattice panel to the back frame,** and then join the front frame to the rear frame with rails H and J. Ease the process by applying glue and then clamping the assembly together as shown. Drive screws to secure the four joints.

5 **Trace the shape of the sink** on the countertop A2. Subtract for the rim, and cut a hole for the sink using a saber saw. Install per the manufacturer's instructions. Bore a hole for the faucet stem, and mount it behind the sink. Attach the countertop to the rails using corner brackets.

2 **Make your own lattice panel as shown,** or buy it ready-made and attach it to the back frame as shown. For an easy way to make your own, draw the lattice pattern on plywood; assemble it with brads and glue; and then trim the ends.

4 **Screw on the top shelf D through rail C.** Fasten the bottom shelf boards K to cleats N with screws. Leave ³/₈-in. gaps between the boards. Screw cleats to the rails G. Finish with primer and exterior enamel paint, and then mount a bar for the hanging utensils.

6 **Connecting the drain to a garden hose** can be accomplished in various ways. Here, the link was made with a piece of bicycle tire tubing, which is attached to the hose with a hose clamp. If necessary, stiffen the end of the hose with copper tubing.

Water Connections

The drain hose, fed through a hole in the lower shelf, can be placed in a flower bed if you're rinsing with clear water.

The faucet is connected to the water supply with a suitable snap-type coupling.

Water Line

Drain Line

1

CHOOSING THE RIGHT SITE

CHAPTER 2

What Should It Look Like?

THE PERFECT PLAN

O nce you have selected the site for your outdoor kitchen, you know the space with which you have to work and whether or not you already have some assets, such as a deck or patio, that will make your job easier.

Of course, you still have plenty to do.

If you are building a new deck or patio for your outdoor kitchen, you will have to determine its size, shape, height, the material you'll use to construct it, and how you will access the house and yard. If you're using an existing surface for your outdoor kitchen, it may need to be upgraded or enlarged. A heavy masonry feature, such as a fireplace or wood-fired oven, for example, will need a concrete slab or footings. You may want to improve access to the house with French doors for better traffic flow, as well.

Whether you're building new or not, it's also time to consider other basic features, such as a roof or some other type of overhead protection, outdoor lighting, a wind or privacy screen, and insect screening. This chapter will help you to make all of these decisions—and give you an idea of what these features are going to cost.

The perfect plan has a lot to do with personal style, but the practical matters described in this chapter are the key to a truly successful plan.

Gauging Costs

As you begin the design process, it's a good idea to know rough costs sooner rather than later. It makes no sense to design your dream outdoor kitchen only to find out that you can't afford to build it. This chart will provide a ballpark idea of what an installed outdoor kitchen will cost, but it doesn't include highly variable costs such as running utility lines. To develop a final budget, you will need a detailed plan upon which to base your estimate. Of course, you can work with a builder who will estimate costs for you.

Stone patio: $15 to $20 per square foot

Patio concrete: $4 to $8 per square foot (add $2 per square foot for decorative treatment)

Deck, PT wood: $15 per square foot

Deck, synthetic: $18 to $20 per square foot

Masonry wood-fired oven: $2,000 to $6,500 (preassembled units; excludes shipping)

Outdoor fireplace: $2,000 to $3,000 installed

Outdoor gas heater: $200 to $800

Outdoor dining table for eight: $750 to $1,800

Outdoor refrigerator: $1,500 to $2,300

Outdoor sink and faucet: $150 to $800

Portable gas grill: $150 to $5,000

Built-in gas grill: $700 to $5,000

Smokers: $75 to $1,000

Arbor (12 x 12 ft.): $1,500 to $3,500

Pavilion with roof (12 x 12 ft.): $2,000 to $5,000

Privacy or wind screen: $10 to $20 per lineal foot

Outdoor cabinetry: $200 to $400 per lineal foot

This custom kitchen, right, required a new patio, footings for the masonry counters, and plenty of custom work—putting the total cost above $15,000.

A kitchen built into an existing space, opposite, will cost less than one built from scratch.

Size, Height, and Shape

Many factors influence the size, height, and shape of an outdoor kitchen. Size, for example, is a function of the available space as well as things such as appliance dimensions and the number of people you plan to entertain. Height may be determined by whether or not you want to keep your outdoor kitchen on the same level as your indoor kitchen, by the view you'd like to have, or by safety issues. Terrain and landscape features often determine shape, but it also has a lot to do with style and aesthetics.

Most successful designs blend with their surroundings. If you plan to build your entertainment area near the house, try extending the existing lines of exterior walls to create a unifying shape. If your house has a sunroom, use similar proportions for your outdoor kitchen. If your kitchen will be away from the house, make it relate to an existing outbuilding or build it around a landscape feature, such as a garden bed. Remote cooking areas can have a more organic shape than outdoor kitchens built next to the house.

Guidelines

- **Square or almost-square floor plans** are more versatile than long, narrow rectangular areas.

- **Outdoor kitchens near the house** will look better if they echo the shape of the house or some portion of the house. For example, if your home has a bump-out, try repeating or incorporating the shape in your outdoor kitchen.

- **Outdoor kitchens away from the house** are more connected to the landscape. They are generally close to grade and may incorporate planting beds and other natural features, such as trees and rocks. As such, their shapes can be more round, polygonal, and organic. Keep in mind that building rectangular shapes generally requires less labor and is therefore less expensive. Laying out organic shapes often requires a professional designer.

- **Build your outdoor kitchen** as close to grade as possible. Doing so will make it less complex to build, safer to use, less costly, less likely to interfere with views from windows and patio doors, easier to make private, and more likely to blend with the house and yard. It will also take up less of your yard with space-consuming stairs.

- **If your outdoor kitchen must be raised off grade,** make it as small as you can while still meeting your needs. Doing so will make it easier to fit with the style of your home and won't put the floor below in perpetual shadow. It will also help keep costs down.

This outdoor kitchen, opposite, creates a good transition from the pool to the house. By picking up architectural details from the house and the pool, the designer has created a kitchen that looks as though it belongs in this setting.

A kitchen placed away from the house, above, can include curves and irregular shapes, such as these opposing, curved counters.

Outdoor Kitchen Space Requirements

• **Dining areas** The table area plus 3 to 4 feet of clearance between the table edge and other elements, such as deck railings and arbor posts, for easy circulation.

• **Snack counters** Allow 24 inches per stool and 15 inches of legroom from the counter edge to the counter support.

• **Grilling areas** The grill/burner area and 3 feet of counter surface to either side or nearby for food preparation; 2 feet of clearance from grill to guardrails, wood structures, and house siding (or as specified by the manufacturer); 4 to 5 feet of clearance for areas subject to traffic.

• **Refrigerators** The area of the appliance and at least 15 inches of countertop to the handle side or on top of the

Allow ample counter space for food prep at both sides of your grill whenever possible.

A grill can go in a corner if the sides and back are insulated. Observe manufacturers' recommended clearances.

fridge. This space serves as a staging area for groceries and platters that require refrigeration. A fridge should also have clearance for the door to swing open and still allow people to walk past the open door. Furthermore, the handle side of the fridge should be nearest the kitchen work area. It should not open into traffic, such as at a back door.

• **Sinks** The area of the sink and 1½ feet of countertop (minimum) to either side of it. The latter serves as a food-prep area and a staging area for washing dishes.

• **Dishwashers** The area of the appliance and at least 2 feet from other appliances. Allow 2 feet between the dish-

washer and a turn in the run of cabinetry.

• **Lounging or sitting areas** The area for each chair or lounge plus about 2 feet of clearance in front of and between chairs. Keep seating well away from the edge of any raised outdoor kitchen floor that has no guardrail, including near descending stairs.

• **Traffic paths** 4 to 5 feet wide between fixed elements.

• **Fire pits, wood-fired cooking appliances, and fireplaces** The area of the footprint, plus manufacturer-recommended clearances between it and nearby structures, such as guardrails and trellises. (One typical gas-fired fire pit recommends a 3-foot side clearance and 7-foot ceiling clearance.) Locate fire features so prevailing winds do not cause smoke to become a nuisance.

Pizza ovens generate more heat than grills. Locate yours away from the house and other structures.

Pavilion protected, the kitchen above has adequate space between appliances and plenty of counter space around the grill and sink.

For easy circulation of traffic, allow 4- or 5-ft.-wide paths around furniture and other features, such as pools, right.

Convenient Access

Before drawing your outdoor entertainment area's floor plan, you will also need to decide how you will access the area from the house and yard. Patio doors are the most practical house-to-outdoor kitchen transitions. They afford a view of your entertainment area and yard from inside your house and come in a variety of configurations. Choose the widest door that will fit into your plan. French doors make roomy, graceful transitions. Adding a second door from the house to an outdoor entertainment area will take the pressure off a heavily trafficked back door.

Size, Height, and Shape Guidelines

Patio doors are available in two main categories: sliders (also called gliders) and hinged. Sliders save space because there is no need to accommodate door swing. If you go for a slider, invest in a quality unit with a secure locking system. A sticky door quickly becomes tiresome, so look for heavy-duty sills and stainless-steel or nylon ball-bearing rollers. Consider a unit with a sliding screen that automatically closes behind you so that you're not constantly asking kids to close the screen door. Today's sliding patio doors are available with wide stiles and rails that mimic the look of French doors. Extra-wide, three- and four-panel sliders are great for opening up your view. There are several types of hinged patio doors. The simplest is a single, one-panel glass door. You can also order a two-panel hinged door with one or two operating panels. With the former, you will have to decide which panel you want fixed. The latter is sometimes called a French door.

Triple-panel doors are also available. Doors can be ordered as either in- or out-swinging. In addition, they can be hinged on the right or left side. You have lots of options, so think them through carefully with a catalog in hand to avoid mistakes. Avoid choosing a door configuration that will interfere with traffic or furniture, such as an out-swing door that blocks access to stairs or an in-swing door that cramps the seating for your indoor kitchen table.

Screen doors complicate matters further. Double patio doors with a single out-swing door, for example, may give you more space inside but often pair with an indoor sliding screen. You may not want the screen frame blocking the wood frame of your new, expensive patio door. An

in-swing version of the same door typically comes with a sliding screen on the outside. Double patio doors with two in-swinging doors, however, will require double out-swinging screen doors, or a single out-swing screen door and one fixed screen panel.

Transitions to the Yard

Access from an outdoor entertainment center to the backyard is not nearly as important as access to the house, but you don't want to impede an impromptu stroll through the garden. Avoid plans where guests may feel

corralled. And be sure to leave clear paths to the garage, basement, or storage shed—the places where you're likely to store spare fuel, maintenance equipment, spare seating, and furniture during the off-season.

Sliding patio doors, above, are the most popular transition from house to outdoor kitchen, especially in areas where doorways must be screened against flying insects.

A four-panel sliding door, right, has no middle barrier, making it easy to transport furniture, kitchen carts, and large trays of food.

Folding Walls

If you have limited space for your outdoor cooking and dining zone, consider a folding wall. It will allow you to share indoor and outdoor space as if it were one room. In effect, both spaces are expanded. Installed between an indoor kitchen and outdoor kitchen, folding walls provide one really large cooking facility with everything at your fingertips. Similarly, you can double or triple the capacity of a dining room by connecting it to the outside with a folding wall.

Folding walls go beyond multiple-panel doors, running the entire length of the wall, with no obstruction to the outside when opened. There are several types from which to choose, including aluminum, wood with aluminum cladding to the outside, and all wood. There is even an all-glass option with no rails or stiles. Mechanically speaking, door panels slide along a top-hung or floor-mounted track and stack separately or fold at hinges for stowage. Keep out insects using a roll-down screen or one that is pleated and slides, or enclose the entertainment area with screens. Installing a folding-wall system is not a weekend do-it-yourself project. Use professional help to ensure that the opening doesn't sag over time and impede opening or closing the system.

Folding walls, left, allow this kitchen to function as both an indoor and outdoor room.

A roof, above, keeps rain from entering the house, even with the folding walls open.

Folding windows bisect the double-wide, indoor-outdoor counter. When the windows are open, opposite, moving dinner supplies and prepared foods in and out is easy.

Folding-Type Open Wall

The main consideration for choosing your folding wall is deciding how the doors should fold. Depending on the manufacturer and model, the doors can fold inward or outward and can accommodate certain angles in the door design. In the long run, you may be better off with a top-hung system versus a floor-mounted one because the top track supports most of the weight and is less subject to dirt and debris than bottom-track systems.

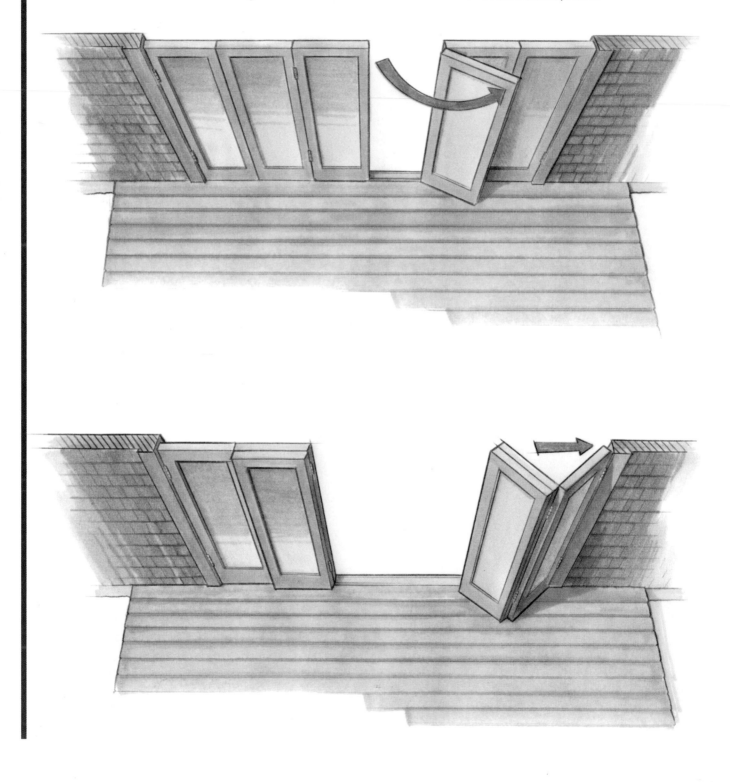

Stacking-Type Open Wall

The advantage to this system is that door panels store completely out of sight into a storage bay (though you will need to make room for this indoors). Slide-and-stack door panels can also handle curves, unlike their folding-wall cousins. Here the choice is made between horizontal or vertical rollers. Horizontal rollers can traverse 90-degree angles, which translates into more stacking options. Units with vertical rollers, however, can be stacked closer together in tighter spaces.

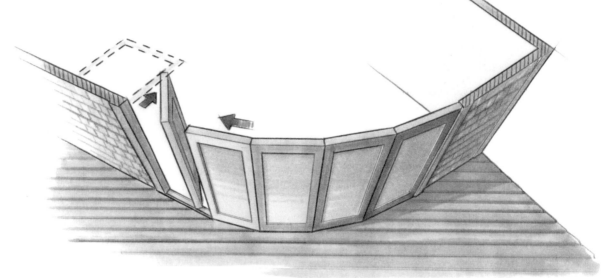

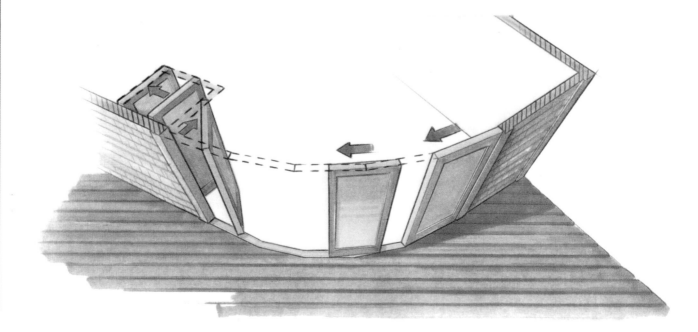

The Primary Work Stations

Your next challenge is to design and place the three primary "stations" common to every kitchen: the cooking station, the food-prep/cleanup station, and the food-storage/refrigeration station. Of course, you may decide to handle food prep, cleanup and/or refrigeration inside, but if you've got the space and budget, save yourself a lot of time by allotting space to them outside near your cooking station.

The cooking station includes your cooking appliances (a grill and side burners, for example), storage for related necessities, and counter space. If your cooking station is heavy, such as a grill that's built into a masonry island, it will likely require a poured-concrete slab and footings.

The food-prep/cleanup station can include counter space, faucet and sink, and trash and recycling receptacles. The counter space should be ample enough for large meat platters and chopping boards. Don't skimp on the sink size either. While bar sinks save space, they're too small for serious work. Trash and recycling containers are best stowed under counters. Look for units that close tightly to avoid problems with flies and other pests.

The food-storage and refrigeration station typically includes counter space, cabinets, and a refrigerator. Situate the counter space so it allows you to easily transfer food to and from the fridge. Your food-storage station should also provide insect- and pest-free food storage for prepared dishes. Shelves covered by insect screening, for example, will keep flies, ants, and other insects away from your baked goodies. Cabinets should be watertight, warp-proof, and fitted with corrosion-resistant hardware. (See page 156 for a complete discussion of outdoor cabinets.) Outdoor kitchen designers typically opt for an under-counter refrigerator. These small fridges allow for a compact kitchen design but don't hold a lot and are less convenient to use—especially in tight quarters. They're also expensive. If you're not ready to spring for one, reserve a space with a shelf for a large cooler. Set the shelf at a height that makes it easy for you to open the cooler and reach inside.

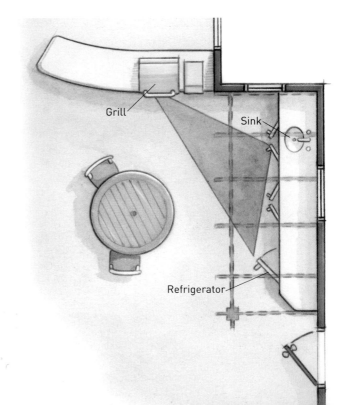

The work triangle, right, is the area bounded by the lines that connect the sink, grill, and refrigerator.

The ample work triangle within this outdoor kitchen, left and below, means two or more cooks can easily share the space. The nearby dining area keeps footsteps to a minimum.

Arranging the Work Stations

Begin with your toughest challenge: the cooking station. It should be out of the traffic flow and not visually obtrusive from either the house or yard. The place you choose should also be big enough for ample counter space for marinade bowls and serving platters on either side of the grill. You'll also want nearby storage for accessories, carving boards, utensils, and cookware.

Other Factors to Consider

- **Prevailing winds** Choose a location for the grill that's normally downwind of the dining area to keep smoke and heavy cooking odor out of your guests' faces.
- **Openings to the house** Avoid placing grills near or under windows, vents, and doors.
- **Overhead combustibles** Grills should also be kept clear of overhangs, including tree branches, patio and porch roofs, eaves, and pergolas. You can usually put a grill under a roof if the area directly above it is protected by a noncombustible vent hood, but check with your local building department for code requirements.
- **Natural ventilation** Try to choose a location that allows air circulation.
- **Direction** Orient the cooking station so you can keep an eye on young children, converse with guests, enjoy a view, and so forth.
- **Electrical or gas lines** If your cooking station will need them, note where the closest access points are.
- **Lighting** Determine whether existing outdoor lighting will be sufficient or if you will need new hard-wired or battery-operated fixtures.
- **Fuel storage** Plan where to store charcoal or wood if your grill or oven requires it.

The Other Stations

Once you have chosen a spot for your cooking station, think about where to put the other two work stations. It may be helpful to envision stocking food, cooking, serving, and cleaning up after an outdoor meal to help you decide where to put things. Again, keep in mind access to water, electricity, and lighting. If you like the relationship of your indoor range, fridge, sink, and counters, perhaps you'll want to arrange your outdoor kitchen in a similar manner—albeit on a smaller scale.

You may also want to refer to commonly accepted arrangements of stations, called work triangles. The triangles refer to work flow (the cook's movement) from station to station. (See the illustration on page 44.) Four common arrangements include galley, L-shape, U-shape, and G-shape. Such guidelines are less important for outdoor kitchen designs because outdoor kitchens are smaller than their indoor counterparts and are not used every day. But the guidelines can be useful. Even a few extra steps from your food-prep area to the cooking station wastes energy and time. More than a few steps from the fridge to the food-prep area does the same.

Don't forget two other important areas in your plan: the dining area and your indoor kitchen. They should be easily accessible to each of the three work stations. You don't want to have to negotiate an obstacle course of counters and appliances to make trips to your indoor fridge or to serve your meals.

Smart Tip Power Up

Work with an electrician to be sure your existing out-door electrical circuit will be able to power your out-door kitchen, including lights, infrared grill burners, refrigerators, and other appliances. If wattage totals are too great, plan to redistribute power to more than one circuit to avoid an overload.

2

THE PERFECT PLAN

A U-shape plan, left, is efficient for a one-cook outdoor kitchen because everything is within easy reach. Be sure you have plenty of space—at least 48 in.—between the opposite rows of cabinets to ensure you have room to move about and to open drawers and doors.

An L-shape plan, especially one with the grill on the short leg, below, offers ample food-prep space for multiple cooks. It's a practical layout that also provides plenty of storage space.

Getting Design Help

Outdoor kitchens, for much of the country, are a relatively new phenomenon. In addition, designing one requires proficiency in several areas. Consequently, getting design help is not as easy as it is for remodeling a bathroom or adding a deck. Few contractors, architects, landscape architects, or kitchen designers specialize in the field.

Even home- and landscape-design software packagers are behind the curve. As of this writing, many have not yet published tools that enable a homeowner to design an outdoor kitchen with a computer. Typically, only full-featured programs intended for design professionals will allow you to tackle such a project, but it takes time to learn the software—and the software is expensive, typically around $2,000.

Sketchup.com, however, does offer a free 3-D modeling tool that enables homeowners to create renderings of many building projects, including outdoor kitchens. A commercial, more powerful version of the software allows you to create scale drawings with dimensions. It will even allow you to see how exposure to the sun changes during the course of a day. See the Resource Guide on page 212.

Manufacturers of essential outdoor kitchen components, such as grills and cabinets, are a source of design help. While many of these services are free, manufacturers often obligate you to buy their goods in return. Nor should you expect the most creative plans from such sources. What manufacturers tend to do well, however, is provide detailed plans for installing products that contractors may be unfamiliar with, such as wood-fired ovens and barbecues.

Tap into all design sources available to you, especially if you're anticipating a complex job. The ideal combination would be to hire an architect or landscape architect for the deck or patio plan, and a certified kitchen designer for laying out the cooking and dining areas. Getting the deck or patio right should be your top priority, as the rest can evolve or be rearranged later.

Drawing up your own building plans is always an option, of course. Even if you plan to hire a professional designer, it's a good idea to collect your thoughts and ideas on paper. The more work you do creating rough drawings and learning about the products you'd like

incorporated in your plan, the more efficiently you'll be able to work with the design professional you hire.

Smart Tip Take Pictures

To envision how your plan will affect the elevation view of your house, photograph the site you've selected with a digital camera. Try to capture a significant portion of the house. Then download the image to your computer and make several printouts. Sketch in details per your plan, including countertops, cabinetry, appliances, and any structural elements. Add plantings, both existing and planned, to give a rough idea of how things will look upon completion.

Seek professional design help if your outdoor kitchen will incorporate lots of new or existing elements, as with the kitchen at left.

Drawings for a Permit

In recent years, more building departments have begun to require homeowners and contractors to obtain building permits for outdoor kitchens. There are at least three types of drawings you'll need. The first, called the site plan, should show your site and its relationship to your house. A scale of 1/8 inch to 1 foot is good for the typical lot. Show property lines and septic areas so the building department can let you know if any setback restrictions apply.

You'll also need a plan drawing. It should show an overhead view of the outdoor kitchen, dining areas, and the portions of the yard and house that connect to them. Plan drawings can be done in a larger scale than site plans; 1/4 inch to 1 foot is typical. Include locations of all utilities in the area, including water mains; sewage, electrical, and gas lines; and storm drains.

Elevation drawings show your project from the sides and front. They can also be done to 1/4-inch scale. If your kitchen is to be built on a sloped grade, you may also need a site elevation. It will show the contour of the existing grade.

Contractors will need drawings of plan details, including framing, cabinetry, overhead structures, stairways, fireplaces, and the like. You may be able to obtain some of these from manufacturers. For example, a wood-fired pizza-oven maker will have details for installing and finishing its product.

Landscaping Can Make a Difference

Plants, trees, shrubs, walls, and fences, as well as careful grading, can make the difference between an outdoor kitchen and entertainment area that sits well in the yard and one that's an eyesore. In general, use hedges and shrubs to help "ground" cabinets and large built-ins, such as grills and walls. Use low plantings, such as garden beds, around your dining area or wherever you'd like to open the view. Vines grown on trellises are a good way to screen unwanted views and to create a sense of enclosure.

When designing the landscape around an outdoor entertainment area, your aim should not be to screen out the yard but to create interesting views. Unless privacy is an issue, plant trees and shrubs at varying distances from the dining area to create a view with depth and interest. Make your yard feel bigger by planting several shrubs that will grow to a large size 10 or 15 yards from the deck or patio perimeter. Plant smaller specimens farther away. Do the reverse to make your yard seem smaller and more secluded.

The lines created by the reflecting pool are carried on by the outdoor kitchen, right and below.

Tuck your kitchen into a corner of your property to make it easier to integrate with the landscape.

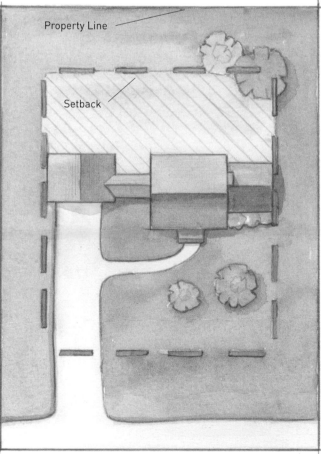

Your municipality typically governs where you can build on your property. You may not be able to build a deck for your kitchen beyond the setbacks of your yard (shown as a dashed line in the illustration above).

Smart Tip Learn the Rules

It's wise to become familiar with building codes, as well as restrictions set by homeowner associations, historical commissions, and zoning departments, before you begin to design the deck or patio for your outdoor kitchen. Some of the key things you will need to know include allowable setbacks (minimum distance of deck from property lines), guardrail and stair-rail height requirements, baluster spacing requirements, and restrictions about being able to see your kitchen from the street in a historical district. Some homeowner associations may even specify architectural styles and finish colors. You may also be required to take out a permit.

CHAPTER 3

Select a Surface for Underfoot

OUTDOOR FLOORS

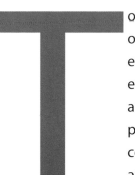

Today, you have more outdoor kitchen foundation or "flooring" options than ever. Wood decking, for example, is now available in weather-resistant exotic species, as well as traditional varieties, such as redwood or cedar. In addition, new types of pressure-treated woods have eliminated health concerns that were associated with wood preservatives of the past. A vast choice of synthetic lumber brands, whether vinyl or a composite of wood fibers and plastic, is also available. They eliminate the need for annual sealing and often for refinishing. The latest offerings have wood graining, come in several colors, and have matching railing systems—but you'll still have to use real wood for structural components.

Cut stone has surged in popularity in recent years. It only needs sweeping or pressure washing to renew it. Brick, tile, and concrete remain perennial favorites, with the latter often your least-expensive option—and available in colors and stamped patterns. Plywood and aluminum make excellent outdoor kitchen foundations, too. The former must be coated with an acrylic polymer. The latter has a baked-on nonslip finish and is lightweight and noncorrosive. Both can be installed to shed rain and keep the space below dry for storage or for additional outdoor living space.

Decks made with composite lumber, such as this one, make good surfaces for outdoor kitchens. To prevent staining, take care to avoid grease drips.

Decks Versus Patios

Wood Decks

- Require regular maintenance
- Dry faster after a rainstorm
- More comfortable to stand on for long periods
- Suitable for outdoor kitchens with portable grills and lightweight fixtures
- Inexpensive if you choose pressure-treated decking
- Easier to raise off grade (allows for second-story outdoor kitchens)
- Great design and style flexibility
- Not fireproof
- Will not last as long as stone or concrete

Masonry Patios

- Require little maintenance
- Better suited to heavy appliances and masonry grill islands
- Inexpensive if you choose concrete
- Expensive if you choose stone
- Not suitable for outdoor kitchens raised more than a few feet off grade
- Limited style choices
- Fireproof
- Extremely durable

Wood Decks

If you want wood decking for your outdoor kitchen and dining area, you've got three choices: pressure-treated (PT) wood (the most common), untreated woods that you must treat yourself, and woods that are naturally resistant to insects and decay. Pressure-treated wood, typically made from pine, hemlock, and fir (with southern pine and Douglas fir being the most common species) is a practical, inexpensive, and durable choice for flooring. It will require a yearly cleaning and sealing to keep it looking good, however. Skip a year or two and you may have to contend with warping, checking, and splintering.

PT wood is no longer plagued by concerns about toxi-city. Today's PT lumber processors have replaced arsenic with copper compounds, such as alkaline copper quaternary (ACQ types B and D) and copper azole (CA-B). The new formulations pose no known threat to humans but may affect marine life. However, copper compounds are highly corrosive to other metals, so hot-dipped galvanized or stainless-steel fasteners are recommended. Steel-framing hardware, such as joist hangers, must also be shielded from contact with ACQ- and CA-treated wood, typically with a self-adhering membrane. PT wood color ranges from dark greenish-brown to light brown, and it can be stained or painted once it's dry.

Untreated woods, such as fir, pine, and new-growth cedar, should be treated with a preservative and require

Masonry surfaces, such as concrete, above, complement outdoor kitchens built with masonry counters and countertops.

Stone floors, right, maintain a rustic look for your outdoor kitchen and are less likely to stain or, if they do, to show stains.

construction techniques that limit the places where moisture can penetrate boards and joints. They are best suited to covered floors, such as on a porch or under a deep eave, as they are subject to rot and insect damage.

Wood that is naturally resistant to insect damage, such as heartwood grades of redwood, bald cypress, and cedar, is good looking and less susceptible to warping, checking, and splintering. Nevertheless, it needs periodic sealing to keep its looks. The primary drawbacks to these woods are limited availability, environmental concerns about over-logging, and high cost. Cedar and redwood, for example, costs two to four times as much as pressure-treated wood. Exotic hardwoods, such as ipe (Pau Lope, ironwood, or Brazilian walnut), teak, Brazilian cherry, and Philippine mahogany, share rot- and insect-resistant characteristics but are generally more difficult to work with than cedar or redwood. Predrilling holes for fasteners, for example, is required because the woods are so hard. This adds to the labor costs. Extra saw blades are also necessary. In addition, some exotics do not take finishes well.

Wood surfaces for outdoor kitchens and dining areas, top right, are less tiring for the legs than masonry floors.

Exotic woods, such as mahogany decking boards, right, require less maintenance than common woods but are more difficult with which to work. For example, pilot holes must be drilled for all fasteners.

Smart Tip Where It Counts

For all premium woods, including redwood, cedar, and exotic species, save money by using them for visible applications only. Use pressure-treated pine or fir for structural components.

Out with the Old

CCA (chromated copper arsenate) pressure-treated wood, its safety rarely questioned for 70-odd years, has been banned. Concerns about arsenic leaching from lumber in decks, playgrounds, and other applications prompted investigations by the Environmental Protection Agency (EPA) and other environmental groups. The studies' results were mixed, but CCA (and other compounds with arsenic) in pressure treatments is no longer available for most residential uses. The EPA has not, however, called for removal of CCA-treated lumber in existing structures.

If you're concerned because you're building your outdoor kitchen on an older, existing deck, use a penetrating oil finish or paint to reduce or eliminate exposure to CCA. Do not use tables built of CCA-treated lumber for food preparation. When removing an old deck, wear a dust mask. Discard sawdust and old boards according to your local laws. Never burn it in fire pits, wood-fired cooking appliances, or fireplaces because this is the best way to become exposed to the arsenic.

Synthetic Decks

Synthetic decking boards make excellent floors for outdoor kitchens, but they are not all alike. Some synthetic products, called composites, combine wood fiber and plastic, often reclaimed from wood waste and recycled plastics. Others are made from vinyl. Both are primarily used for decking, but many manufacturers also offer matching components for guardrails and handrails. Synthetic trim boards and moldings are also available. Neither composites nor vinyl materials are recommended for structural components, such as joists, posts, or beams.

Synthetic products have some advantages over the real thing, as well as some drawbacks. They are not subject to rot or checking and won't splinter. They come precolored, so they don't need finishing upon installation. Some types are easier to bend, lending themselves to handsome railing designs and decking patterns. Synthetic wood's big selling point is that you don't have to seal it every year to keep it looking good.

On the other hand, synthetic lumber products are expensive—often as much or more than top-quality wood products. Despite cosmetic improvements, synthetics don't quite look or feel like wood either. Some brands are not as easy to work with as wood because of their weight and density. Composites will "weather" (fade or turn gray) and need to be refinished if you want to maintain the original color. Dense types of synthetic lumber hold more heat than real wood, causing discomfort to bare feet. They also get dirty, can stain and scratch, and will support the growth of mold and mildew—though not as readily as wood. Although it can be argued that synthetic lumber saves natural wood resources, some are not environmentally friendly and, in the case of vinyl-based products, are a source of hazardous pollutants during their manufacture.

It's easier to curve trim boards with composite lumber than with real wood.

Smart Tip Do a Test Drive

Not all composite boards are created equal. Some accept fasteners cleanly, without mushrooming or breaking the end grain. Others don't. Ask your supplier for recommendations, or take home samples and check them out yourself. While you're at it, check for resistance to stains and scratches as well.

Composite boards enable designers to create decks with organic, yard-fitting shapes, top.

Most producers of composite decking boards also produce matching vinyl components for guardrails, above.

An intricate floor pattern, left, is easier to execute with prefinished synthetic deck boards.

Alternative Decking Materials

Two decking materials that are often overlooked when choosing a floor for an outdoor kitchen are aluminum and plywood. Aluminum is low maintenance, lightweight but strong, prefinished, cool underfoot, recyclable, and has a clean, contemporary look. The planks are substantial enough so that denting and noise are not problems. Built-in channels between the planks carry away rain, so no additional under-deck drainage system is needed should you want to put a patio below an upper-level outdoor kitchen or use the space for storage. Aluminum decking is well suited to harsh seaside climates and for use with roof decks. Matching aluminum guardrails and handrails are also available.

Plywood decking has a more formal, less busy appearance than traditional decking products. Waterproofed properly, it provides a dry space below. One system involves caulking and taping all joints and then rolling on several coats of acrylic polymer. Once cured, it forms a flexible but tough skin on the plywood that is suitable for normal deck traffic. Granules can be added to the last coat to add texture and improve skid resistance. Ideal for creating a deck over a flat roof, this product also can be used to weatherize a traditional wood deck. A second system achieves roughly the same effect but with a heavy vinyl membrane that you roll in place. The seams are overlapped and heat welded. Likened to an outdoor vinyl sheet flooring, it's available in various colors, patterns, and textures.

Aluminum decking is easy to maintain and can be recycled, unlike most wood and composite deck products.

Applying an Acrylic Polymer Finish

1 Before applying an acrylic polymer deck coating to a plywood deck, seal all joints with caulk.

2 Use a trowel to smooth caulked areas so that they are flush with the plywood.

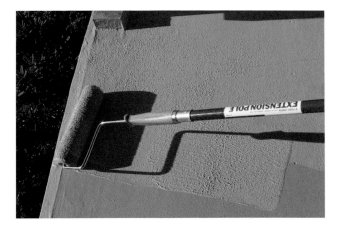

3 Apply two thick coats to the entire decking surface using a thick nap roller.

4 To ensure watertight joints, embed joint tape in polymer as specified by the manufacturer.

5 Mix texture granules into the final polymer coating for a slip-resistant surface.

6 The cured coating offers a tough finish with a pebbly texture.

3

OUTDOOR FLOORS

Stone Patios

Dimensional landscaping stones, such as bluestone and sandstone, have become a popular outdoor surface in recent years. Like wood, their natural look fits with most backyard landscapes. Stone suits many styles, from rustic to contemporary. Unlike wood, it requires little maintenance and is nearly impossible to damage.

Shifting is rarely a problem with large stone pavers, and edge constraints are unnecessary (as they are with small concrete pavers and brick). If a root or frost heave does shift a paver, it's relatively easy to reposition. Nor does stone prevent water from reaching the roots of perimeter trees or shrubs, as do concrete patios and brick bedded in concrete. Need to fix a broken water main or run an electric line? Just pry and lift the pavers out of the way.

One drawback to a stone floor is that it's tough on the legs if you stand on it long enough. It's expensive to install, but much of the cost is labor. So if you have a strong back and a helper, it is a job you can tackle—and you'll save a lot of money in the process. Finally, stone is not nearly as versatile as wood or other decking materials. Unlike a deck, which can be built to any height you need, stone must rest on the ground. Of course, it is possible to raise the grade with gravel, but this can be costly. A stone floor can also be uneven, so it may not be the right choice for the elderly or small children.

Flagstone, set in a mortar base, blends well with this stone-clad grill counter, above right.

Interesting patterns for laying stone pavers are numerous and add interest to an outdoor kitchen, opposite.

Smart Tip Save Prized Trees

Avoid laying a stone patio where it will significantly encroach upon the root zone of a prized tree. Most of a tree's roots are within the top 6 inches of soil. Cutting these roots for excavation may eventually kill or damage the tree.

Buying Dimensional Stone

Stone pavers are available in stock sizes, ranging from 12 x 12 inches to 4 x 6 feet and in thicknesses from 1 to 2 inches. Landscape designers generally recommend at least 1½-inch nominal stock to ensure that your patio will not shift or break. In many situations, where drainage is good or rainfall light, thinner stock can be used. Cost ranges from $4 to $7 per square foot plus delivery charges. When purchasing bluestone, it's wise to handpick each piece in the yard. Otherwise you may end up with significant variations in color, thickness, width, and length. Order enough to cover the area (in square feet) plus 5 percent for breakage and repair. For estimating crushed-stone needs, multiply the area's length by its width (in feet), and then multiply by .33 (⅓ of a foot, or 4 inches). Divide by 27 to get cubic yards. For tons, multiply the result by 1.6.

Laying a Stone Patio

Before starting, gather goggles, earplugs, a dust mask, work gloves, and knee pads. You'll also need the following: a sturdy contractor's wheelbarrow, level, measuring tape, spade, shovel, steel garden rake, rubber mallet, masonry wet saw, and a hand tamper or vibrating plate-tamp compactor.

Stake twine to indicate the edges of your planned outdoor kitchen area. Be sure the corners are square. Temporarily lay out two rows of the stone you plan to use, one along the patio length and the other along its width. If possible, adjust the dimensions of the patio so all stones in a row are full width. Doing so eliminates the need to cut them to fit and will save a lot of time. Remove the stones and excavate the patio area to a depth of about 5 inches below the grade. Tamp or run a plate compactor over the excavated area.

Fill the excavated area with about 4 inches of stone dust (crushed stone), and level using a garden or landscaping rake. A 4-foot level taped to the edge of a straight 2x4 makes a good leveling tool. Tamp the stone dust to a height of about 2 inches below grade. Compaction is important to ensure that your stones do not shift. A vibrating plate-tamp compactor will speed the job. It's quite heavy, so you'll need a hand truck or helper to move it, but once in operation the machine moves with relative ease. Make at least three passes over the entire stone dust base. You may use sand and gravel as the bed for your patio instead of stone dust. It does not compact quite as well but will do the job. If you're going this route, lay down 3 inches of gravel and then 1 inch of sand before proceeding.

Select a corner and carefully lay the first stone so its edges align with the twine guidelines. The first stone is critical because all other stones will be placed in reference to it. Stones can be laid in a wide variety of patterns and are typically set about 1 inch apart. When all stones are laid, sweep stone dust, sand, or small pebbles into the joints. Wide joints can be planted with a hardy groundcover.

1 Excavate to a depth of 5 in.; tamp if the soil is loose; and level. A 4-ft. level taped to a straight board makes a good leveling tool.

4 Check the compacted depth. You want to leave a bit more than the thickness of the stone from dust to grade. Then toss on a thin layer of loose stone dust.

7 Use a rubber-mallet handle to compact the dust under the edges of the stones. You can also use a rubber mallet to seat the stone.

2 Distribute stone dust to a height of about 1 in. below grade, and rake until level. A landscape rake (shown) will speed the job.

3 Compact the dust by making several passes using a plate compactor. For best results, select a compactor that sprays water as it goes.

5 Expect bluestone pavers to have irregularities on one or both faces. Trowel the loose dust (and compacted dust if necessary) to conform to the underside of the stone.

6 Lay down the paver, best side up, and check that it is at grade height (using the guideline installed earlier); then level the stone. A spacer stick creates uniform spacing.

8 If it's necessary to cut stones, rent a masonry wet saw. Connected to your garden hose, it will keep the dust to a minimum and the blade cool so it lasts longer.

9 Toss a few shovelfuls of stone dust on the finished job, and use a broom to sweep it into the gaps. After several weeks, once the stone dust has settled, repeat.

Concrete Patios

Concrete makes a very serviceable outdoor kitchen floor, all the more so because it can be colored and stamped to simulate a variety of materials, including stone, slate, tile, and brick. Although it has the same comfort negatives as stone, it's less expensive to install and just as easy to clean. If your outdoor kitchen is larger than 50 square feet, it makes sense to hire professionals to pour a concrete patio. They own all of the necessary equipment and can assist you in choosing a distinctive decorative finish. If that's not in your budget, however, you can do the job yourself. The products needed for acid etching are available at many home centers. Be forewarned: installing a concrete slab for an outdoor kitchen requires physical strength and carpentry skills.

Installing a Concrete Slab

The site must be marked and excavated to a depth of 8 to 10 inches. Then it needs to be leveled and filled with a 4- to 6-inch layer of gravel. After compacting the gravel, you'll need to build a form around the edges, and haul and mix dozens of bags of premixed concrete. (A 10 x 10-foot area will require about 50 bags.) Renting an automatic mixer from your local home center will save some strain, but you'll still need to move the wet concrete from the mixer to the site, one wheelbarrow at a time. Next comes leveling the wet concrete (slide a straight 2x4 along the top edge of the forms) and finishing (smoothing) the surface with a bull float and broom. And don't forget to install reinforcing welded-wire mesh before the pour, to cut in control joints afterward, and to finish the edges. Doing so will help keep your patio crack free.

Concrete is a versatile material that can be made to look like stone, brick, or tile. The acid-etched and polished concrete surface, left, gives the appearance of polished stone.

The concrete floor, right, was scored before it cured to give it the look of stone or tile.

Concrete Slab

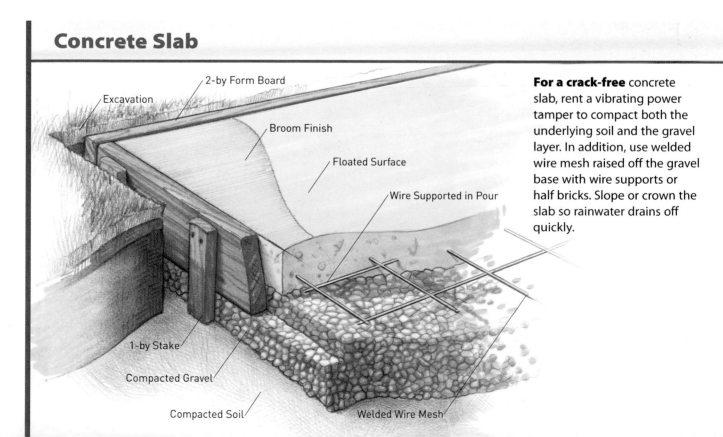

Excavation

2-by Form Board

Broom Finish

Floated Surface

Wire Supported in Pour

1-by Stake

Compacted Gravel

Compacted Soil

Welded Wire Mesh

For a crack-free concrete slab, rent a vibrating power tamper to compact both the underlying soil and the gravel layer. In addition, use welded wire mesh raised off the gravel base with wire supports or half bricks. Slope or crown the slab so rainwater drains off quickly.

Tile and Brick

Depending on the style of the outdoor kitchen you're planning, tile or brick may be your outdoor flooring solution. Both tile and brick can be installed over an existing or just-poured concrete slab. (See the illustration on the opposite page.) If using tile, be sure to choose a nonglazed, outdoor grade for slip-resistance and to avoid chipping and cracks in freezing weather. For a traditional brick look, choose 4 x 8 brick pavers made from fired clay. For a more contemporary look, consider concrete brick, which is available in a wider variety of sizes, shapes, and shades. Both tile and brick can be adhered to concrete with a concrete bonding agent and thin-set mortar. Keep in mind that paving bricks are thicker than tile ($1\frac{1}{2}$ to $2\frac{3}{8}$ inches), so your initial excavation will need to be deeper. Use grout to fill the joints.

Brick, either of concrete or clay, can also be installed over a base of crushed stone and sand. Despite the fact that this approach will require a perimeter frame of wood or stone blocks, it is more forgiving for the novice do-it-yourselfer than brick installed over concrete.

Concrete combines with traditional brick—laid in a running-bond pattern—for this elegant edge, above.

Concrete pavers, below, are available in several colors and may be installed dry over a crushed-stone base.

Brick can be installed in many patterns, including this herringbone design, opposite.

Mortar-Laid Brick Patio

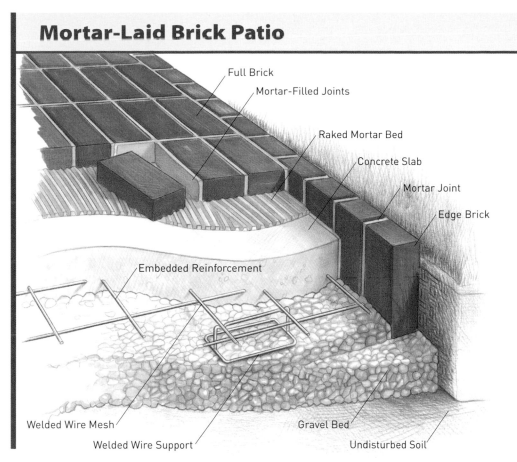

Full Brick

Mortar-Filled Joints

Raked Mortar Bed

Concrete Slab

Mortar Joint

Edge Brick

Embedded Reinforcement

Welded Wire Mesh

Welded Wire Support

Gravel Bed

Undisturbed Soil

Brick can be laid in many patterns. Layout suggestions are available online or from your masonry supplier. When you're ready to mortar brick to your concrete slab, make a dry layout first, placing the bricks in the pattern you have chosen. Once you're satisfied that they will fit properly, remove the bricks; apply a layer of mortar; and rake using a notched trowel. Do not trowel on more mortar than you can work before it begins to cure.

CHAPTER 4

Protection from the Elements

IMPROVING COMFORT

Even rugged outdoorsy types cry "gimme shelter" when confronted with cooking and dining under a blazing sun, downpour, or cool, stiff breeze. So, now is the time to consider all the ways you can make your outdoor soirees a little less dependent on the weather.

Overhead protection from the sun and rain should be a top priority in many climates. Protection will also keep the countertop, appliances, and furniture cleaner, reducing cleanup time prior to using your kitchen. You may also want to consider wind protection in the form of a wall or windbreak. Whether built or planted, it can make a huge difference on gusty days. Privacy may be an issue, too. It can be handled with outdoor shades or with something more permanent, such as a fence. If insects are a plague to you, a screened enclosure may be indispensable.

Still not quite at home in your kitchen away from home? Manufacturers now offer a boatload of creature comforts, including outdoor carpeting, propane patio heaters, evaporative coolers, and even high-tech mosquito repellers. The following pages will lay out your options.

An arbor is an attractive way to create shade. Grow flowering vines or install fabric panels if you need additional shade.

Shelter Options

Houses with porches or deep eaves provide natural shelter for outdoor cooking and dining, but unless you're fortunate enough to have one—or unless you're planning to design and build a new home—you're going to have to find a different solution. One possibility is an outdoor kitchen closet. This only works if you have some extra space inside your home, such as an indoor kitchen with room to spare, a walk-out basement, or a room at the back of a garage. The benefits of outdoor kitchen closets are that they are well protected from the weather, easy to maintain and winterize, unobtrusive, and relatively inexpensive to build.

Roofed Structures

A roofed structure is the most permanent solution and can often be designed to fit right in with your home's architecture. The roofing material can range from asphalt shingles or roll roofing to polycarbonate or fiberglass panels. A framed roof can sit atop a porch addition or it can be freestanding and supported by a gazebo or pavilion. Keep in mind that structures attached to the house are easier and less expensive to build than those that are not.

Detached Structures

Pavilions and gazebos are typically detached from the house. They can be screened-in or not. While it requires a bit more engineering to build a stable freestanding structure (the main structure cannot act as an anchor), detached structures are often pleasing focal points for the backyard landscape. They also offer a sense of getting away from it all.

An attached structure offers the best protection for an outdoor kitchen. The connected porches, below, include roofed, screened, and open options, opposite bottom left.

An outdoor closet tucked into a deep eave, left, is a simple and low-cost way to house an outdoor kitchen. Bifold doors hide cabinets and appliances when they aren't in use.

A large gazebo, below, is another good way to house an outdoor kitchen. Run counters and appliances around the perimeter. Use the central area for dining.

Do-It-Yourself Pavilion

A pavilion, such as the one shown here, allows you to dine outdoors in greater comfort. It protects you from the blazing summer sun and from rain showers. Position it where there's a good view of your gardens and not too far from your cooking area. Because it's compact—less than 65 square feet—it will fit in a modest-size yard. Nevertheless, it easily accommodates four diners. The size can, of course, be increased should you need a larger pavilion.

Site Preparation

Level an area for the pavilion, and use twine and stakes to mark the corners. You'll need a 4-foot level, a long measuring tape, and a bit of high school geometry to get it right. (Two diagonals of equal lengths, intersecting at their midpoints, will automatically give you a perfect square or rectangle.) Then dig four holes for the post footings. You may either pour the footings using a tube-type form or, if the soil drains well, use partly buried concrete blocks. The four posts will rest on the footings. This designer used concrete pavers or brick, laid on 4 inches of stone dust, for the floor.

This compact dining pavilion can be a focal point for nearly any backyard landscape. Use 6 x 6 pressure-treated wood.

D-I-Y Pavilion Materials

A: 4 pcs. $5^1/_2$ x $5^1/_2$ x $79^1/_2$ in.*
B: 2 pcs. $1^1/_2$ x $5^1/_2$ in. x 8 ft. $10^1/_4$ in.*
C: 4 pcs. $1^1/_2$ x $3^1/_2$ x 52 in.
D: 3 pcs. $1^1/_2$ x $5^1/_2$ x $75^1/_2$ in.
E: 2 pcs. $1^1/_2$ x $5^1/_2$ x $86^1/_2$ in.
F: 12 pcs. $1^1/_2$ x $2^1/_2$ x $25^3/_4$ in.
G: 18 pcs. $1^1/_2$ x $2^1/_2$ x 18 in.
H: 15 pcs. $1^1/_2$ x $2^1/_2$ x 5 in.
J: 6 pcs. $1^1/_2$ x $2^1/_2$ x $75^1/_2$ in.
K: 4 pcs. $1^1/_2$ x $2^1/_2$ x $41^3/_8$ in.
L: 6 pcs. $1^1/_2$ x $2^1/_2$ x $82^1/_2$ in.
M: 2 pcs. $3/_4$ x $1^1/_2$ x $86^1/_2$ in.
N: 4 pcs. $3/_4$ x $3/_4$ x 50 in.*
O: 3 pcs. $3/_4$ x $3^1/_2$ x $75^1/_2$ in.
P: 2 pcs. $5/_8$ x $16^1/_2$ x $75^1/_2$ in.
Q: 2 pcs. $3/_4$ x 48 x $86^1/_2$ in.

R: 3 pcs. 36 x $85^1/_2$-in. rolled roofing
S: 4 pcs. 5-in.-dia. x 24-in. concrete piers

Miscellaneous:
8-in.-dia. x 4-ft. forms for concrete piers (4)
40-lb. bags concrete mix (16)
$3^1/_4$ x $5^1/_2$ post bases (4)
2x6 joist hangers (6)
Rolled roofing (1 roll)
10.3-oz. tubes roofing cement (4)
$3/_4$-in. roofing nails
No. 6 screws ($1^1/_2$, 2, $2^1/_2$ in.)
No. 8 screws (3 in.)
Primer
Paint

* Long-point measurements; require additional cutting

N

C

C

N

A

A

$13\frac{1}{2}$"

$13\frac{1}{2}$"

B

B

$2\frac{3}{8}$"

E

R

E

$2\frac{3}{8}$"

K

L

A

K

L

Q

M

L

R

P

C

O

B

D

S

D

A

S

C

S

$1\frac{1}{2}$"

C

C

$16\frac{1}{2}$" $15\frac{5}{8}$"

4"

P

4"

4"

$2\frac{3}{8}$"

B

$9\frac{7}{8}$" A

$75\frac{1}{2}$"

A $9\frac{7}{8}$"

8'$10\frac{1}{4}$"

$1\frac{9}{16}$"

$11\frac{5}{8}$"

E

A

A

A

79$\frac{1}{2}$"

1"

75$\frac{1}{2}$"

1"

5" 25$\frac{3}{4}$" 5" O 25$\frac{3}{4}$" 5"

G 5" J G

18" H F H

H 5"

D 5" J

12$\frac{3}{4}$"

2" H

2"

1 Cut the posts as shown in the drawing; then begin chamfering the post corners by making a 45-deg. cut using a handsaw.

2 Cut the rest of the chamfer using a jigsaw. It is about 1 in. deep as measured from the post corner. Sand the chamfered edge to rid the post of splinters.

5 Join the sides together, and brace in place as shown. Screw the railings in place.

6 Assemble the gables as shown, making the decorative end cuts using a saber saw.

9 Install the roof framing using galvanized screws.

10 Install plywood roof deck with screws. Preinstall molding M along the exposed sheathing edges. Begin roofing at the eaves and finishing at the ridge.

3 Assemble the three railings using screws, beginning with the H-shaped middle parts and working outward.

4 Cut post-top angles, and plane the top edge of the beam E to match the post-top angle. Then assemble the side frames using framing hardware and screws.

7 Attach the gables to the posts using long screws. They will be further supported with roof framing later.

8 It's much easier to preassemble the 2 x 3 roof framing on the ground.

11 This is the completed corner assembly, viewed from the inside.

12 Finish the roof with the triangular moldings N. Prime and paint the moldings prior to seating them in a bed of roofing cement.

A large side-arm umbrella screens a big area and allows easy movement of furniture and people beneath it.

Shade Umbrellas

Keeping a sunny outdoor living space cool during the hot months is no easy task, but creating some shade will definitely help. The simplest approach is a center-post umbrella that's designed to fit through a hole in a dining table and into a base below. If you go this route, buy a large umbrella that's 8 to 12 feet wide and easy to open and close. Octagonal units will give you more shade than square units of the same width. You'll want a heavy base to keep the umbrella anchored when the wind blows. Alternately, buy a post base that bolts securely to your deck or patio. Be forewarned, however, that a fixed umbrella position may not handle your outdoor entertainment area's changing shade patterns.

Side-post umbrellas get the post out of your way and come in even bigger sizes. The umbrellas mount on an arm or hang from a boom that can rotate 360 degrees to block the sun as it crosses the sky. The most-expensive units have a tilting mechanism. Check with your manufacturer's instructions to ensure secure deck mounting in windy conditions. Post-less umbrellas can be hung from an overhead structure, such as an arbor or pergola. Such units are raised and lowered with a pulley.

Choosing an outdoor fabric for umbrellas is about looks, durability, and light transmission. Several types are on the market, including acrylic canvas, PVC fabric, and high-density polyethylene (HDPE). Acrylic canvas and PVC are best for water resistance. HDPE is best for blocking UV rays in hot, arid climates but typically is not water resistant. Check that the fabric you select is treated to resist mold and mildew, too.

Post-less umbrellas, left, hang from an overhead structure, such as an arbor or pergola, and can be removed when not needed.

When buying a center-post umbrella, below left, opt for the largest diameter possible. You and your guests will be less likely to have to continually dodge the sun.

Both center-post and side-arm umbrellas, below, can be mounted to a wood deck or concrete surface. The former may require the addition of blocking below the deck boards.

4

IMPROVING COMFORT

Other Shade Solutions

Other outdoor-room covering options include awnings and shade cloth. Awnings are either manually or electrically powered; they attach to your house and provide protection from both the sun and the rain. Stretch shade cloth over the outdoor entertainment area using cables or secure it over a structure, such as an arbor or pergola. Both awnings and shade cloth are more versatile than framed roofs; simply roll them up when you don't need them. Fabric solutions are also a great way to add color to your backyard retreat.

Freestanding gazebos, fitted with outdoor fabric, will also offer respite from the sun. Lightweight units offer portability, while heavier structures are semipermanent and may require special support framing or their own footings. Either can be draped with fabric for privacy and screened for insect protection.

Shade sails, aptly named because they look like sailboat sails, are an innovative way to add shade and contemporary styling to an outdoor dining area. Held together by stainless-steel cable sewn into the edges, the triangular or rectangular sails attach to posts or to the existing structure with steel rings at reinforced corners. Consult with a professional to find the sail configuration best suited to your climate and needs.

Freestanding fabric gazebos, below, are a quick, inexpensive way to provide shelter for a dining area.

Retractable shades, mounted between the bays of an arbor or pergola, opposite top, are your most versatile shade solution, though they won't help much in the rain.

Shade sails, attached with cables to buildings or trees, opposite bottom, provide shade with no posts to get in the way. They can also be attached to posts when necessary.

Shade-cloth panels, left, can also be attached to an overhead structure. The panels, which can be removed for an annual cleaning, provide protection from ultraviolet rays.

Canvas canopies, below, span greater lengths than other solutions and are easier to remove when the time comes. Posts are supported by sleeves affixed to large, steel baseplates.

4

IMPROVING COMFORT

Trellises, Pergolas, and Arbors

Trellises, arbors, and other overhead shade structures can give your outdoor kitchen and dining area a lush, secluded feel while reducing glare and heat from the sun. Use trellises to create flowering walls that can shelter you from wind and sun. They can offer a degree of privacy as well. Morning glories, clematis, climbing roses, and jasmine are good choices. Use arbors to create outdoor ceilings laced with greenery. Be sure to design your arbor to carry the weight of more heavy, vigorous vines, such as wisteria, trumpet vines, climbing hydrangea, and grape. If you're not into the care and maintenance of vines, consider a retractable canopy for your pergola or arbor. It discreetly installs along tracks on rafters, providing shade without interfering with the style of the structure.

This kitchen and dining area, right, is sheltered from the sun by a pergola and a wall trellis.

A pavilion, opposite top, unlike an arbor or pergola, has a solid roof. The walls may be left open or partially closed.

The pavilion's interior, opposite bottom, is protected and boasts recessed lights, a ceiling fan, and a fireplace.

Shade Structures

Trellis

Pergola

Smart Tip Plan Ahead

Don't make the addition of a pergola, arbor, or large trellis a design afterthought. In all likelihood, it will need to be anchored by footings—a tougher task once the deck or patio is built.

Arbor

Insect Control

There are several approaches to keeping insects out of your outdoor kitchen and dining areas. The surest is screening. It can be used to protect porches or detached structures, such as gazebos. The traditional approach to screening an outdoor room is to fasten screen panels between the posts of a framed, roofed structure. This can be expensive, especially if you're planning a large kitchen-dining area. Rather than build a structure that protects your entire outdoor entertainment center, you may opt to screen off the dining area only. For a screened room on a deck, be sure to screen gaps in the decking.

Other methods to suppress insect activity in the cooking area include repellents and traps. Misting is a relatively new nontoxic repellent. Tiny droplets of water, shot from nozzles mounted around your patio or deck, deter mosquitoes and other flying insects. Misting systems can also be used to deliver insect repellents such as citronella. Keep in mind, however, that the primary purpose of misting systems is to cool the air on hot days. (See page 88.) If your insect activity is during cool weather, misting may be of limited value to you.

Traps work by luring insects away from where you and your guests are dining to a device that captures and kills them. Electric bug zappers of the past, which used light as the lure, were noisy and didn't discriminate between good and bad insects. New products take a different approach. For example, research shows that mosquitoes are attracted to carbon dioxide, heat, and moisture, all of the stuff you exhale. Some new "zappers" use propane to produce the same mix, but when the mosquitoes fly toward the device, they're vacuumed into a net where they dehydrate and die. Other devices operate without propane, using light, color, heat, movement, and odor to lure their prey. Manufacturers claim that these mosquito eliminators can protect up to an acre.

Prefabricated Screen Houses

Prefabricated screen houses, or screen enclosures, are an economical way to protect an outdoor kitchen from flying insects. Models come in many different sizes in order to cover nearly any deck or patio. You can also opt to cover only a portion of your cooking and dining area. Models are either freestanding or three-sided, attaching to the house on the fourth side. Many are sold in kits for do-it-yourself installation and can be installed in a single afternoon, assuming you've already attended to the foundation.

The best units have heavy-gauge aluminum frames with a baked-on enamel finish. Units that have galvanized-steel framing, whic is finished to resist fading and oxidation, are less expensive. Roofs are often constructed of vinyl fabric in a wide range of vinyl grades and thicknesses, from 6- to 22-ounce weights. Heavy-duty versions will handle moderate snow loads and have aluminum roofs with polystyrene insulation. If considered a permanent structure, as some are, you will need a building permit. Lighter-duty roofs should be taken down during winter months if you live in a snowy climate.

Screens are a necessity in many areas. Hanging out in this screened room, left, with its floor-to-ceiling openings, is almost like sitting outdoors.

A prefabricated screen room, right and below, comes with all framing, glazing, and screening materials. You supply the concrete slab. Note: this model can be installed as a sunroom, a screen room, or both. Combination windows allow you to switch from one to the other, depending on the season.

Smart Tip — The Net Result

Mosquito netting is graceful and romantic looking. It can be installed as curtains around porches or detached structures. Available in seamless lengths up to 900 feet and 12 feet high, mosquito netting will also provide protection from no-see-ums, flies, bees, and many other pesky insects.

IMPROVING COMFORT

4

Windscreens

Controlling wind, especially if you live in an area where it blows much of the time, is one of the trickier problems to solve. That's because wind does not always act as you would expect. A solid wind barrier for your outdoor kitchen, for example, may cause wind to curl over the wall and swirl at you from behind. The solution is to build your wall so that some wind will filter inside. A wall built with a lattice panel set into the upper section is one option. Spacing the boards of a fence or wall an inch or two apart is another. Designers sometimes use tempered- (heat-treated) glass panels set atop guardrails to reduce wind and preserve a desirable view at the same time. Thicknesses range from $\frac{1}{4}$ to $\frac{1}{2}$ inch and are typically set into commercially available aluminum guardrail systems. Outdoor fabrics can be effective as well, as long as you don't mind the flapping sound when the wind gets gusty.

Tempered-glass panels installed over a solid guardrail offer stiff resistance to wind without blocking the view.

Windscreen

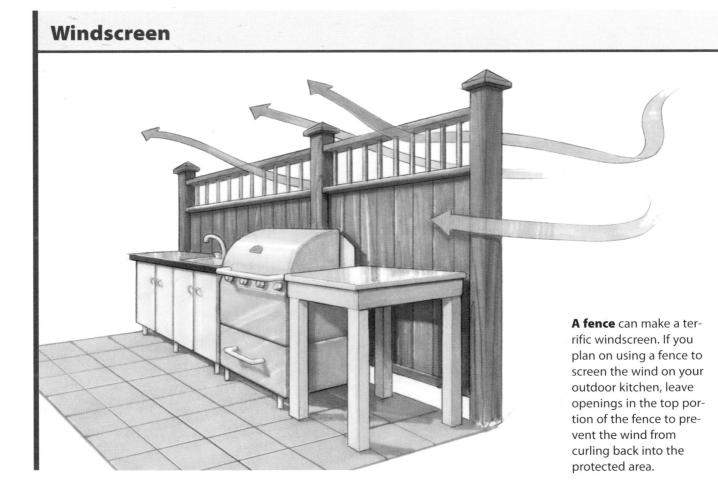

A fence can make a terrific windscreen. If you plan on using a fence to screen the wind on your outdoor kitchen, leave openings in the top portion of the fence to prevent the wind from curling back into the protected area.

Deck Shades

This design couldn't be simpler. Extend guardrail posts to the height desired for privacy, and then make the shades as shown. To raise the shade, roll from the bottom and secure with elastic loops. Use elastic loops to secure the shades to hook screws in the down position.

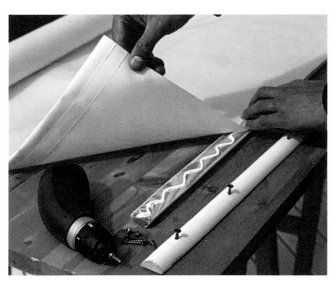

1 Fashioned from outdoor fabric, the shades are reinforced by sandwiching the bottom edge between half-round trim pieces. Secure it using caulk and screws.

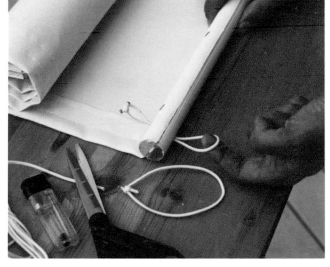

2 Bore two holes through the glued-up half-round. Then thread the elastic loops through the holes; tie them; and melt the cord ends to prevent unraveling.

3 The shade top, reinforced with two flat pieces of trim, receives two loops of elastic that hold the rolled shade in the up position.

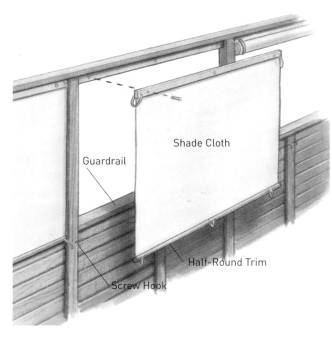

Shade Cloth

Guardrail

Half-Round Trim

Screw Hook

Heating and Cooling

There are several ways to maintain a comfortable temperature in your outdoor entertainment area. To add heat, install a fireplace or fire pit. They contribute adventure and romance to the scene as well. On the minus side, burning wood means you'll have to deal with smoke, firewood, and ash. If you want something a bit more convenient, consider a patio heater.

Patio Heaters

Patio heaters come in several shapes, but parasol-shaped models are the most popular because they can be moved. Find them at outdoor furniture stores and on various online shopping sites. Costs average about $300, although tabletop units are available for less than $100. Be sure to read the product information on what type of fuel the heater takes (kerosene, butane, propane, or natural gas) and the radius of heat it will project. The patio heater should also include various safety features, including emergency cutoff valves, flame controls, electronic ignition, and even infrared heating technology. Whichever model you decide to purchase, place it in a wind-sheltered area and keep it a safe distance from children.

Outdoor Coolers

For warm climates, there are outdoor coolers. They work on the principle of evaporative cooling. That is, as water evaporates it lowers air and skin temperatures. For example, residential misters create a fog of tiny, hair-thin droplets via strategically placed nozzles. As the droplets evaporate, air temperatures can drop up to 30 degrees F. Residential misters work best when the humidity is under 40 percent, although they will provide some relief with higher humidity. At 70 percent humidity, one manufacturer says its mister can reduce temperatures from 90 to 82 degrees F. Residential misters come in high-, mid-, and low-pressure systems. The higher the pressure, the greater the cooling coverage. Prices range from less than $50 for a low-pressure kit to more than $2,000 for a high-pressure system that can handle large areas.

Misting fans, which are often used on the sidelines to cool NFL players, are another option for lowering temper-

Ceiling fans, right, and ceiling-mounted heaters can be used to control the temperature in roofed kitchen enclosures.

Outdoor fireplaces, below, are, of course, another way to stay warm when it gets nippy outside.

Outdoor Cooling System

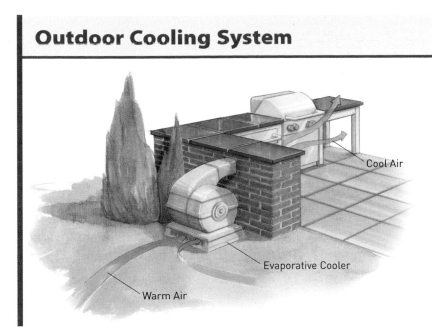

Cool Air

Evaporative Cooler

Warm Air

Evaporative coolers, either installed behind a wall, above left, or placed in the garden, left, can lower the temperature in the surrounding area by as much as 10–30 deg. F, depending on the conditions.

Propane-fueled heaters come in many styles, including the floor model shown above.

atures via evaporation. Nozzles feed a fine mist to a fan. As the mist evaporates, the fan-blown air is cooled. The fan breeze contributes to making people feel cooler as well. Low-pressure, hose-fed misting fans can cool small patios by up to 25 degrees F, depending on humidity. Larger, high-pressure misting fans can cool areas of 400 square feet and more. Residential misting fans come in a wide range of shapes and sizes—some designed to look like lampposts—and range in price from $135 to $1,850.

Many misting devices control insects in addition to providing cooling. The fogging action itself is a deterrent. If that's not enough, many units can be used to disperse

natural insect repellents, including pyrethrum and citronella. Other benefits of misters are improved plant health and dust control.

Portable evaporative coolers are yet another outdoor cooling option. A large fan, mounted in front of a panel of water-absorbing fluted pads, draws moist air through the pads and distributes it in the area to be cooled. Although big and visually intrusive, these units can cool large areas efficiently. They are mounted on wheels for portability. Units begin at about $900 (with wheels and stand) and can drop temperatures 18 to 22 degrees F over a 600-square-foot area, according to the manufacturer.

CHAPTER 5

Create an Accident-Free Zone

SAFETY AND HEALTH

An outdoor kitchen is a great place to create culinary delights for family and friends, but unless you attend to safety, it can be a recipe for disaster as well. Flammable gas fuels, hot grease, open flames, and intense heat make for a volatile mix. Gas grills alone account for hundreds of fires and about 30 serious injuries each year, according to the Consumer Product Safety Commission (CPSC). Electricity, especially when combined with a wet environment, can be deadly. Even relatively innocuous accidents, such as trips and falls, can lead to tragedy. In many outdoor kitchens, there are stairs and steps to negotiate, often in low-light or high-glare situations. Adequate safety rails, balustrades, safe stair design, and outdoor lighting are essential. In addition, precautions are necessary wherever food is to be prepared. Work surfaces must be easy to sanitize. Perishable foods must be kept cool. Flies and other disease-spreading pests must be kept away. If children are present, precautions must be taken to lock away alcohol, cleansers, cutlery, and other hazardous items. On the following pages, you'll learn how to ensure healthy, accident-free outdoor living.

Electrifying a complex outdoor environment, such as this one, takes skill and experience. Use a licensed electrician to help ensure safety.

Grill Safety

To minimize the chance of grill mishaps, the CPSC recommends that users check gas cylinders for leaks. Supply hoses should be checked, too, for wear, sharp bends, and proximity to hot surfaces or dripping grease. Clogged tubes that feed gas to burners cause most fires, especially on grills that have not been used for some time. After a long period of disuse, clear tubes of insect or grease blockage with a pipe cleaner or small brush prior to igniting the burners. (See below for more recommendations.)

Your best defense against burns is to place the grill away from traffic and to instruct children to stay at least 3 feet away at all times. The cook should have insulating mitts, as well as long-handled grilling utensils to keep hands well clear of flare-ups. To minimize the likelihood of clothing catching fire, do not wear loose-fitting garments while you're working at the grill.

Grills Under Roofs?

There are good reasons to place your grill under a roof, especially if you live where it rains a lot. Your equipment will stay cleaner and last longer. While standing at the grill, you'll be better protected from the elements, too. Many municipalities, however, restrict grills from being placed under a roof. The CPSC and National Fire Protection Association (NFPA) agree. They say that grills should be kept at least 10 feet from any building and that they should not be used in a garage, carport, porch, or under a surface that can catch fire. According to the NFPA, grills cause 900 home-structure fires and 3,500 outdoor home fires each year. Most of these, however, are caused by portable grills with old, poorly maintained gas cylinders and fuel lines—not new models with permanent gas hookups. In addition, the use of range hoods and nonflammable ceilings improve safety. Check with your local building department before finalizing your plans.

Grill Safety Tips

- Follow the manufacturer's instructions that accompany the grill.
- Observe recommended clearances from combustible materials.
- Never leave a grill unattended.
- Never store or use flammable liquids near a grill.
- Place your grill on a stable surface so it won't tip.
- Place your grill on a nonflammable surface, such as stone or concrete, that's at least 10 feet from the house, garage, and trees.
- Keep a fire extinguisher at hand and have a nearby garden hose attached to a spigot while your grill is in use. Or keep a 4-gallon bucket of water at hand.
- Replace scratched or nicked gas cylinder connectors, which can eventually leak gas.
- If you detect a gas leak, immediately turn off the gas at the tank. Don't attempt to light the grill until the leak is fixed.
- Keep lighted cigarettes, matches, and open flames away from a leaking grill.
- Never use a grill indoors because it produces deadly carbon monoxide.
- While lighting a grill, keep the top open. If the grill does not light in the first few attempts, wait five minutes to allow gas to dissipate.
- Never attempt to repair the tank valve or the appliance yourself. See an LP dealer or a qualified appliance repairman.
- Use caution when storing LP tanks. Always keep tanks upright. Never store a spare tank under or near the grill. Never store a full tank indoors.
- To avoid incidents while transporting LP tanks, transport the tank in a secure, upright position. Never keep a filled tank in a hot car or car trunk. Heat will cause the gas pressure to increase, causing the relief valve to open and allowing gas to escape.
- Check the CPSC Web site (www.cpsc.gov) for callbacks that may affect your grill.

With proper venting, above, grilling under the roof of an outdoor kitchen won't cause smoke to build up and the ceiling to discolor. If you install a range hood, size it properly for your grill or you may not solve smoke problems.

A well-lit grill, left, will help prevent accidents—and will allow you to respond quickly should they occur.

Traffic Safety

Be generous when sizing the main traffic "corridors" of your outdoor kitchen and entertainment center. (See the illustration on the opposite page.) Allow at least 4 feet so that the traffic lanes can accommodate two people walking abreast. Also allow at least 4 feet around activity areas where people will circulate, such as a dining or conversation area. Locate potentially hazardous activity areas away from traffic corridors. For example, put the cooking area away from the traffic corridor. Ditto for tripping hazards, such as stairs and fire pits. You may use benches, planters, and trellises to define traffic paths. A small counter may be all you need to force kids to walk around a grilling or dining area rather than through it. For outdoor rooms built on decks, use built-in benches and planters to help keep visitors from stepping off edges that have no guardrails.

Smart Tip Safe Cooking

The United States Department of Agriculture (USDA) has four recommendations for handling food safely: clean, separate, cook, chill. Wash your hands thoroughly. Keep raw meat away from cooked foods. Cook foods to a high enough temperature to kill bacteria such as E. coli and salmonella. Refrigerate or freeze perishables, grilled foods, and leftovers within two hours.

Plan for Safe Traffic

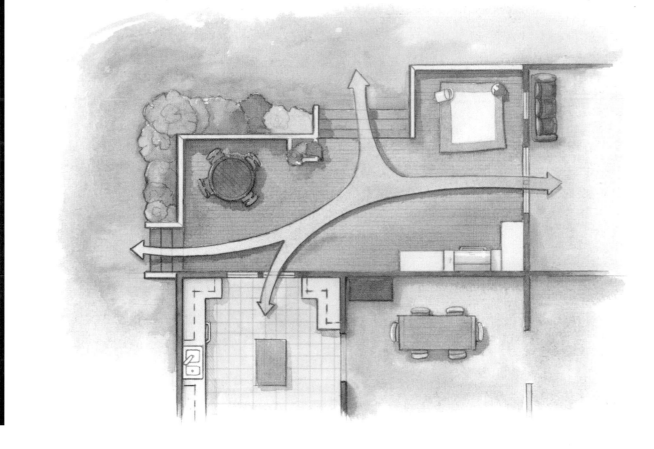

Ensuring Sanitary Conditions

An outdoor kitchen is vulnerable to both natural and man-made contaminants. Control natural contaminants, such as bacteria and bird and insect droppings, by using easily sanitized work surfaces and by keeping food covered and cool. Surfaces that receive the National Sanitation Foundation's NSF 51 rating are approved for use in commercial food-prep areas. Easier to disinfect because they are nonporous, they include stainless steel, solid surfaces (plastic materials such as Corian), and engineered stone (quartz). Other weather-resistant surfaces can, of course, be used but will require more elbow grease to

This plan, opposite top, leaves guests plenty of room to navigate an active pool, spa, and bar area.

The grill at the far end of the porch, opposite bottom, is well out of the flow of traffic, reducing the risk of accidents.

root out bacteria. The NSF recommends cleaning surfaces with warm, soapy water before and after each use. A final rinse of 10 percent white vinegar is an especially effective disinfectant. The NSF also recommends countertops with coved backsplashes, which are easy to keep clean.

Man-made contaminants are not always so straightforward. It almost goes without saying that you should not use or store insecticides near food. Pesticides and herbicides, as applied by many lawn care services, can be a problem as well. A common ingredient in many herbicides, 2,4-D, has been the subject of many cancer studies and is considered a possible carcinogen the Environmental Protection Agency. You probably don't want any on your lamb kabob. Switch to organic, nontoxic lawn care programs wherever possible. Organic weed deterrents are made from grain, beets, molasses, vinegar, and soaps, with corn gluten meal being the most popular. As a bonus, the corn gluten also serves as a slow-release fertilizer.

Safer Stairs

Outdoor kitchens often require one or more transitions from one level to another. If they're only a stair or two, just be sure they can be seen, are not too close to a door, and have a generous tread width. If the transition requires more stairs, state and local building codes will define the variables. They include handrail requirements, riser height, stringer width (for stairs built of wood), and baluster spacing. In general, you will need handrails for any stair with more than three risers. They must be fully graspable and between 34 to 38 inches high, as measured from the tread nosing. The maximum riser height is typically 8 inches and the minimum tread width is 9 inches. Typical combinations include 6- to 7-inch risers and 10- to 12-inch treads. For safety, wider treads are better. For comfort, the rule of thumb is that twice the riser height plus the tread width should equal 26 inches. The narrowest dimension for a stringer (the wide, angled board that supports stair risers and treads) after cutouts for the treads and risers have been made is usually 3½ inches. Baluster spacing is the same as it is for guardrails: less than 4 inches. For safety reasons, many building codes also limit the number of stairs in a single run. (You can't fall as far if you trip.)

Stair and Railing Safety

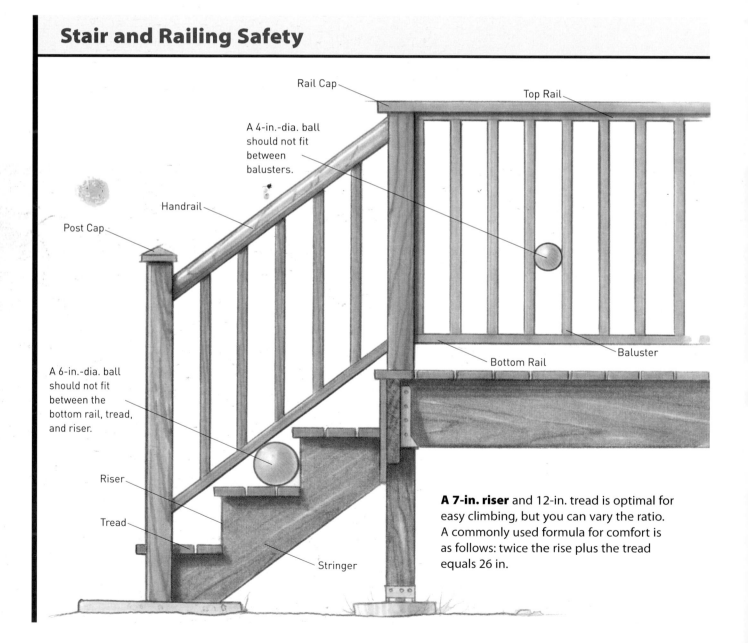

Rail Cap

Top Rail

A 4-in.-dia. ball should not fit between balusters.

Handrail

Post Cap

Baluster

Bottom Rail

A 6-in.-dia. ball should not fit between the bottom rail, tread, and riser.

Riser

Tread

Stringer

A 7-in. riser and 12-in. tread is optimal for easy climbing, but you can vary the ratio. A commonly used formula for comfort is as follows: twice the rise plus the tread equals 26 in.

Smart Tip Safe Landing

Allow ample space for landings at doors. You should not have to step backward off a landing in order to open a door. Small landings, unless used with sliding or in-swinging doors, are hazardous—especially when you are carrying platters of food and cooking supplies to the deck or patio. Preferably, the platform for an out-swinging door should be 2 feet deeper than the door width.

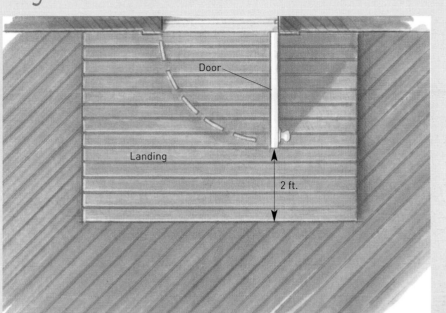

Door

Landing

2 ft.

This glass-paneled gate, above, matches the deck railings and is an ideal solution for homes with young children.

Stainless-steel cable rails, right, provide minimally obstructed views. They are typically installed horizontally but can be done as vertical pickets if so desired.

Lighting for Safety

If you plan to use your outdoor kitchen and dining area during the evening, consider installing safety lighting at stairs and along floor perimeters that have no guardrail. General lighting, either around the outdoor kitchen perimeter, on posts, or attached to the house, will also help prevent accidents due to trips and falls. Many outdoor lighting manufacturers make safety-lighting products designed especially for outdoor rooms. Some install directly in stair risers or stringers. Others go under railings or atop balustrade posts.

To illuminate a sizable entertainment area and the yard beyond for reasons of security, floodlights—mounted to the house, a pole, or a tree—are a good solution. Look for models that offer motion detection and energy-efficient lamps, such as compact fluorescent or metal halide. Some models will wirelessly activate other house lights and sound a chime inside the house when someone is approaching. Other floodlight models include a motion-activated, wireless color video camera. Be sure to avoid positioning floodlights in ways that will cause glare to your neighbors.

Lighting, especially at minor level changes and around seating, above, can improve your outdoor kitchen's safety at night. It will help prevent guests from taking a spill the next time you host a party after dark.

A specialty drill bit, right, is used to make holes for stair-riser light fixtures. Low-voltage light fixtures, below, are easy to install, but seek advice from the manufacturer about the transformer size you'll need.

Candles and torches are an option, but electricity can't be beat for convenience. There are a variety of 120-volt and low-voltage wall-mounted and hanging fixtures, right, available at home centers and lighting stores.

Lights at stairs make navigating the outdoor entertainment center, below, much safer at night.

When gas lines are buried under a masonry floor, use tracer wire so they can be located if necessary.

Gas and Electrical Safety

Installing a gas line, if your home has natural or propane gas service, eliminates the need for constantly refilling cumbersome propane tanks. No longer will you run out of gas midway through cooking a meal. The line can be connected to the gas line in your house via a "quick-connect" fitting—assuming gas is available to you. Have your gas line installed by a certified technician. It should include proper pipe burial, tracer wire (so it can be quickly located in the future), and a shutoff valve located near the grill so you can turn off the gas when the grill is not in use.

Electricity always requires caution, but in an outdoor kitchen, where people often stand directly on the ground in a wet environment, this is especially true. If, for example, an outdoor refrigerator develops a ground fault (current unintentionally leaking to a grounded surface) and the user touches it while standing on a wet patio floor, the user's body may provide a path to ground for the current, causing severe injuries or death from electrocution. Consequently, all outdoor outlets should be GFCI protected. GFCIs protect against dangers associated with ground faults, as well as with short circuits and overloads, by immediately cutting the flow of electricity when a variation in current is detected. All work should be done by a licensed electrician and should include cable burial, proper grounding of appliances, underground feeder (UF) cable, a breaker inside the house at the start of the underground wiring circuit, the use of protective conduit as specified by code, and waterproof equipment.

Properly installed gas lines for a fireplace, above, and a grill include shutoff valves that can be easily accessed in an emergency.

A gas-fired fire pit, below, is better suited to deck areas than those that burn wood.

Smart Tip Douse the Fire

A fire in an outdoor kitchen can involve several types of materials, including grease, paper, plastics, and electrical equipment, so opt for a multipurpose fire extinguisher. When it comes to extinguisher size, the bigger the better—but don't buy one so big you can't handle the weight easily. Store the extinguisher in a cabinet near the grill. Do not put it inside the grill cabinet, where it might be unsafe to reach should a fire erupt.

PART 2

CHAPTER 6

SELECTING APPLIANCES

When it comes to food preparation, what's more fun than cooking outdoors? Friends and family gathered together, enjoying flavorful food, makes grilling, in a word, great.

Our love affair with backyard cooking took off in the early 1950s when George Stephen, a Chicago welder, created the Weber Kettle, a domed charcoal grill. It allowed folks in the Windy City to cook over even heat, without generating too much smoke. A decade later, Illinois' Walter Koziol, whose company manufactured gas lamps, invented the gas grill.

Today, the grill remains the focal point of most outdoor kitchens. Eight out of every ten households in the United States own a grill. And, of course, today it's a big business with seemingly limitless options, from the simple tabletop hibachi to a high-end infrared grill built into a beautiful stone grill island.

Choosing the right grill for your outdoor kitchen can be overwhelming. This chapter will help make the task a little less daunting. You'll also get a look at other appliances and accessories, including ovens and refrigerators, that will help you make your outdoor kitchen complete.

This outdoor kitchen has it all. It includes a grill, a warming drawer, a charcoal cooker, a refrigerator, an ice machine, and a bar center—and a breathtaking view.

Choosing a Grill

The grill is the heart of your outdoor kitchen—and it may end up being its most expensive component, too—so choosing the best one is an important decision. Grills come in all shapes and sizes. Before you invest your hard-earned money, make your decisions about the following:

Grill Types

Will your outdoor kitchen feature a built-in grill or one that stands on its own? A grill that's built into a countertop or grill island usually has more cooking capacity and plenty of work area on each side. A freestanding unit on wheels, on the other hand, is better if you want to be able to move your grill, either to clear the area when you're not cooking or to move the grill to a more optimum position when the weather or season changes.

Fuel Options

Gas—natural gas or liquid propane (LP)—is by far the most popular choice here. For flavor, however, many traditionalists won't go near a gas grill, instead favoring a charcoal unit. Electric and pellet grills are other options. (For more on making the proper fuel choice, see "The Fuel Types" on page 112.)

Size

This refers to the size of the cooking surface. To determine how big your grill should be, think about how you plan to use it. Are you a weekend griller who will be cooking for your small family? If that's the case, a grill with a surface area of 300 to 450 square inches should suffice. A bigger family might require a grill with 450 to 600 square inches of cooking area. If you plan to host large neighborhood parties, invest in a grill with a cooking area that's at least 600 square inches. The types of food you cook are important when determining grill size as well. Rib roasts and shish kabobs take up a lot of space. Burgers and hot dogs are more compact.

Btu

A Btu (British thermal unit) is a standard measure of energy, but it isn't a true measure of a grill's cooking

Freestanding grills, such as this 623-sq.-in. model with fold-down side shelves, come fully assembled.

power or heat output. A Btu rating is a measurement of how much gas the grill can burn per hour. More important than a high Btu rating is the ability of a grill to reach and sustain desired cooking temperatures—and this depends on a number of factors, including size and heat distribution. A large grill with what seems like an impressive Btu rating, for example, may not perform well if the ratio of Btu to area is inadequate. In general, grills with two burners should produce 30,000 to 50,000 Btu, or about 100 Btu per square inch of cooking surface. Burners should be designed to spread heat evenly to all areas of the cooking surface.

Construction

Look for a durable unit. You don't want a model that rattles when you shake it. Most of the top grills today have bodies made of heavy-duty cast aluminum or stainless steel. If you're going with a freestanding unit, make sure the wheels roll easily—and that they lock, too. You'll likely have to fork over a bit more now for a solid, sturdy grill, but with proper care it should last many years.

Assembly

How easy is it to put your grill together and get it ready for

This built-in gas grill is wide—53 in.—but it still fits snugly into one end of this compact outdoor kitchen.

outdoor entertaining? Most folks don't want to bring a new unit home and find out it takes an engineering degree to understand the novel-length owner's manual. Take some time in the store to get an idea of what prep work is required. The best brands reduce the amount of assembly required. Look over the manual to see if it's going to be easy to follow.

Accessories

Some people prefer the bare-bones approach, while others want every accessory known to man. Most will fall somewhere in between. Figure out what you want out of your grill, and then determine which "extra" is a must. Perhaps a built-in rotisserie has to be included. Maybe you can't do without a removable smoker box. The grill of your

choice doesn't have to come prepackaged with every accessory you may want. (To get an idea of what accessories can be added later, see pages 114 and 115.)

Service

If a part breaks, will it be easy to replace? If you need troubleshooting help, is a toll-free hotline available 24/7?

Warranty

You're going to invest hundreds of dollars—maybe even thousands—in your grill, so you want to know you're covered should something go wrong. Most major manufacturers stand behind their products; many offer warranties that cover parts and labor for one to five years and burners for a lifetime.

Grill Features

If your repertoire is limited to burgers and hot dogs, there is no need to go all out on a top-of-the-line unit. If you're an avid griller, however, you'll want to consider a unit with superior features. Here are some:

Igniters

Many gas grills are ignited with a knob or a push button. The knobs give off two or three sparks per turn, while buttons give off one spark with each push. The best—and most reliable—choice is a battery-powered electronic igniter, which produces continuous sparks as long as the button is held down.

Burners

These are the workhorses of the grill, providing the gas and flames. Most grills come with steel burners, although some are stainless steel, cast iron, or cast brass. The latter three tend to last longer because they are not subject to rust. Look for a grill with more than one burner; having only one burner may result in hot and cold spots on the cooking surface.

Infrared Burners

Want a higher, more intense heat? If so, you'll want to consider a grill with infrared burners or invest in a stand-alone infrared burner. (Some gas grills combine infrared and standard burners in one unit.) Unlike traditional burners, infrared burners do not require a secondary heat element, such as ceramic briquettes, which means less heat will be lost. Infrared burners concentrate the flames through a ceramic tile that has thousands of microscopic holes. This process converts the fuel into infrared energy. The intense heat—and the lack of a secondary heat element to trap drippings—keeps flare-ups to a minimum.

Grates

Don't overlook this important part—it's where meat meets fire! Grates should be strong and sturdy, provide good heat transfer, and have a nonstick surface. Most gas grills have stainless-steel, cast-iron, porcelain-coated cast-iron, or porcelain-coated steel grates. Stainless steel provides an even heat distribution and will work well for a

long time, but it will not hold the heat as well as cast iron. Cast iron requires more maintenance; you need to keep it cleaned and well oiled to avoid rusting. Porcelain-coated grates are rustproof and easy to clean, but they can chip.

Radiants

Sometimes referred to as heat diffusers, radiants, which are located between the burner and the grate, evenly distribute heat and vaporize drippings. The most common radiant is lava rock. Lava rock is irregularly shaped and doesn't hold heat evenly. It's also porous, which allows grease to build up. When not changed regularly, flare-ups are possible. Pumice stone is similar to lava rock but is less porous, resulting in fewer flare-ups. Ceramic briquettes cost more than lava rock and pumice stone but distribute heat more evenly and are self-cleaning. Long-lasting metal bars provide even heating and the fewest flare-ups, because food drippings are vaporized as they contact the hot plate.

Drip Trays

Excess drippings must be properly channeled away from the burners to avoid flare-ups or, even worse, a grease fire.

Infrared burners are ready to grill in a matter of minutes and cook twice as fast as a standard burner.

Burners, such as the "E" burner, left, need to be replaced more often than most grill parts, so look for ones with warranties for 10 years or more.

Grates with closely spaced bars, below, make it less likely that food will fall through them. These grates are made of heavy-duty stainless steel.

6

SELECTING APPLIANCES

A good drip tray covers the entire cooking area, won't stick or catch when opened and closed, and should be accessible from the front of the grill. The deeper the tray, the less often it needs to be emptied and cleaned. If you plan on purchasing a charcoal grill, be sure it includes a removable ash-collection tray for easy cleanup.

Shelves

Many freestanding grills include exterior shelves that flip up (usually from the side) or are fixed, offering additional space for food prep. These shelves are usually made of plastic, but some are cast aluminum or stainless steel.

Grill Anatomy

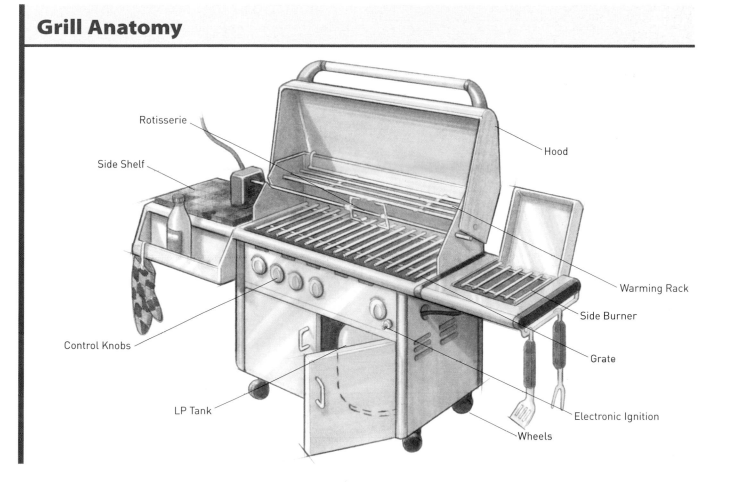

Rotisserie

Side Shelf

Hood

Control Knobs

LP Tank

Warming Rack

Side Burner

Grate

Electronic Ignition

Wheels

Grill Price Categories

You get what you pay for. That's the general rule of thumb when you buy almost anything, including a grill. Here's what to expect when you're grill shopping. Note: these are general guidelines, not hard-and-fast rules.

Basic

The basic grill, ideal for serving four to six people, has a small grilling area with one burner (maybe two) that has one control. Most of these no-frills grills have enameled-steel housing, with plated-steel or chrome-plated aluminum cooking grates. You'll be hard-pressed to find any stainless-steel parts or accessories in this category. Most basic grills cost $100 to $300.

Midrange

This is the best choice for most people. The

This midrange grill, above, has three stainless-steel burners, a 12,000-Btu side burner, porcelain-enameled cast-iron grates, and a painted-steel frame.

This basic grill, left, offers 308 sq. in. of surface area, two burners, and porcelain-coated grates.

This high-end grill, opposite, is a freestanding unit with stainless-steel grates. It includes three 22,500-Btu burners, two 15,000-Btu side burners, and a 14,500-Btu infrared burner.

grilling area is larger and includes two or more separate burners, which allows greater control of heat. The burners are backed by longer warranties (often 10 years or more). Most midrange grills have a cast-aluminum or stainless-steel housing, though the stainless steel may be of the 400 series, which has less corrosion-fighting chromium than the 300 series. The premium grates are often coated with porcelain enamel. The majority of grills in this category include electronic ignition, a side shelf, and perhaps a rotisserie or a smoker tray, but not many more extras. Most midrange grills cost $300 to $600.

High-End

The top-of-the-line grills have more burners (often five or six) that provide more heat. The burners have a lifetime warranty, and often an infrared burner is included in place of a traditional burner. The housing is 300-series stainless steel. The grates

may be, too, though some are cast iron. Grills in this category come standard with all sorts of accessories—side burners, smoker trays, rotisseries, and storage compartments, among others. High-end grills, which are often stylish and aesthetically pleasing, will last a lifetime. And they should, considering they can cost anywhere from $600 to $5,000 or more.

Smart Tip When to Buy

Don't wait until a week before your big Fourth of July party to go grill shopping. Head to your local home-improvement center or specialty retailer—or check out some of the Web sites listed in the back of this book—at the end of the outdoor cooking season to get the best deals.

The Fuel Types

Food may be the fuel you need to power your body, but you won't get food from an outdoor kitchen until you decide what kind of fuel-powered grill to buy. Gas grills are the most popular, followed by charcoal units, and pellet grills may be the wave of the future. Electric grills are also an option.

This charcoal grill uses a gas assist to light the coal fast, combining the tradition of charcoal with the ease of gas.

Gas

The numbers don't lie. Gas grills are by far the most popular grill type. According to the Hearth, Patio & Barbecue Association, 71 percent of grills owned in the United States are of the gas variety. Gas grills offer push-button ignition, quick preheating, and a steady heat supply that is controlled with the simple turn of a knob. There are no fires to stoke or ashes to empty.

A gas grill is simply a grill that uses gas from a tank or a natural gas line for fuel. The grills are fueled by liquid propane or natural gas—not both. Some manufacturers offer conversion kits, but there is no easy way to convert your grill from one fuel type to another. Be sure to select a grill that accepts your fuel source. Liquid propane is typically stored in cylindrical tanks and is almost always located on a shelf below or hung on a bracket beside the grill. You can expect to get 20 to 30 hours of use from a full tank. Natural gas-fueled grills do not require tanks, so the possibility of running out of gas during cooking is eliminated. They are permanently hooked up to your home's natural gas supply. Excluding installation costs, natural gas is about half the cost of propane to operate.

Charcoal

A charcoal grill is basically a receptacle for coals with a cooking grate above it. The principle fuel is either natural lump charcoal or charcoal briquettes (compacted ground charcoal, coal dust, and starch). Natural lump charcoal burns hotter, which means you use less. Briquettes produce more consistent heat, but many people feel charcoal imparts a better flavor. Ah, flavor. That's the reason many people own charcoal grills. These units, which are generally the least expensive, are the choice for purists who want to barbecue (a long, slow heating process), not grill (cook quickly, directly over high heat). The coals—and the smoke they create—provide flavor that many barbecue enthusiasts swear by.

Charcoal grills have come a long way since the hibachi dominated the market 30 years ago. Today you can find anything from a hibachi to a kettle grill (a round or nearly round unit with a domed lid that typically stands on three legs) to a large, powder-coated steel model. Built-in charcoal grills are not as readily available as their gas counterparts, but the number keeps rising.

Pellet

You may not have heard of these yet. If gas prices surge again, you will. Small wood pellets provide the fuel source and infuse the food with flavor from the smoke. The pellets, which are stored in a hopper, are available in a variety of flavors, including mesquite, hickory, apple, and alder. (The latter is great for fish.) They can be fed into the firebox at variable rates—slower for barbecuing food, faster for grilling. Pellet grills are increasing in popularity thanks to their energy efficiency and their clean-burning properties. The grills—and the wood pel-

GAS VERSUS CHARCOAL

Here are some of the basic pros and cons of gas and charcoal grills. Take a look, and then decide which grill fits the bill.

Gas Grills
- Easier to turn on
- Heat up in about 10 minutes
- Have a steady heat supply
- Provide even heat
- Offer greater temperature control
- Produce great-tasting food
- Generally more expensive
- Straightforward food prep
- Relatively easy to clean and maintain

Charcoal Grills
- No push-button ignition
- Heat up in about 20 minutes
- Coals must be replenished
- Burn hotter
- Not as easy to control temperature
- Produce great-tasting food with distinctive flavor
- Generally less expensive
- Thrill of cooking with a fire
- More cleanup involved

An LP tank, above left, even when it's empty, weighs as much as 18 to 20 lbs. This full-extension drawer makes it easy to replace the tank when it runs out of gas.

Pellet grills, left, are safe—there are no gas leaks or smoldering briquettes to cause worry. This model automatically augers wood pellets to accurately provide three different cooking temperatures.

lets—are not widely available yet, so they tend to be the most-expensive grill choice.

Electric

Electric grills make up only a tiny fraction of the barbecue market, and they can be more difficult to find than the other types of grills, but they may be worth a look. Electric grills, available as built-in or freestanding units, are easy to operate and maintain. They are also ready to cook in the shortest amount of time. An electric grill is often smaller than its gas and charcoal counterparts, so it may be more suited for those living in an apartment or a condominium. But even then it may not be the best choice. Many argue that the flavor an electric grill imparts doesn't come close to what a charcoal or gas model produces.

Smart Tip The Leak Test

Use water and dishwashing soap to test for gas leaks on a propane tank. In a well-ventilated area, away from any heat source, brush the soapy water on the tank—don't forget to apply it on all hose and valve connections. Turn on the tank. If any portion is bubbling, a leak is present.

Grill Accessories

You've selected a grill. That's the first step. Now it's time to outfit your grill. What you get will depend on your budget and your cooking style. If you want to turn your grill into a multifunctional cooking center, consider the following items:

Side Burner

If you plan on preparing an entire meal outdoors, a side burner is a must. It allows you to boil a pot of water for corn or lobster, heat sauces, or stir-fry vegetables, eliminating the need to run back inside again and again. Look for one with two burners in a single unit with a continuous grate, which will allow you to use large pots and pans.

Warming Rack

Temperature drops considerably as the distance between the cooking surface and the burner increases. A warming rack is simply a shelf, often removable, located above the main cooking surface that keeps food warm. Many can be adjusted to two or three different levels.

Rotisserie

For slow, even cooking, consider buying a rotisserie. This is a motorized spit (a long metal rod) that suspends and slowly rotates food over the grate. The rotisserie is a popular grill attachment because it slowly roasts, creating foods crispy on the outside and tender and juicy on the inside. The more weight the rotisserie can handle, the better—the best can accommodate at least 40 to 50 pounds. Keep in mind that a rotisserie requires an electrical outlet for the spit motor.

Pizza Stone

Pizza stones sit directly on the cooking grate, using the grill's high heat to produce pizzas with crisp crusts and hot, bubbly toppings. The stone holds heat and helps create a simplified version of an Italian brick oven. Pizza stones work great for flatbreads and calzones, too.

Smoker Box

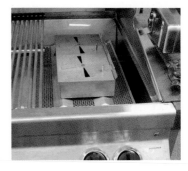

These perforated metal containers hold wood chips and give a smoky flavor to your food. Also known as smoker trays, smoker boxes are positioned on a gas grill's lava rocks or ceramic briquettes, or on a charcoal grill's grate. Removable smoker boxes are included with most high-end grills, but some are built in as part of the cooking grate. Wood chips come in all sorts of flavors, from apple and maple to mesquite and pecan.

Wok Ring

This accessory is for stir-fry fans. A wok is a bowl-shape utensil used for stir-frying vegetables, shrimp, or pieces of meat to create Asian-inspired dishes. A wok ring is a stainless-steel ring that positions the wok properly on a regular burner.

Griddle

Would anyone like breakfast? Set a nonstick cast-iron griddle on the grate to cook the perfect pancakes or crepes. Some griddles are two-sided; they cook the pancakes and crepes on the smooth side and use the grooved side for preparing bacon or sausage.

Grill Basket

This is a must-have item if you want to grill whole fish, veggies, and other fragile foods. A hinged wire basket with a latch allows you to flip the food with no mess, making searing your favorite filet incredibly easy.

Vegetable Rack

Use a vegetable rack to keep food such as potatoes and corn away from direct contact with the grill.

Thermometer

If your grill doesn't come with a built-in thermometer (often hood-mounted), you may want to consider one. A thermometer, which is most useful if you are smoking or slow-cooking food, will provide approximate grilling temperatures and help control the heat more precisely. To be sure your meat is cooked at just the right temperature, however, the gauge needs to provide specific, accurate information. Remote-control models have a receiving unit that you can carry around with you—it will beep when the food is done.

Tool Set

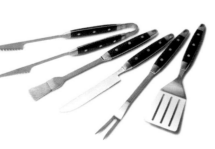

No matter what you're cooking, it's necessary to have the right tools on hand. Any utensil set for grilling should include a spatula, fork, tongs, knife, basting brush, and grill-cleaning tool. Stainless-steel tools with long, durable handles are recommended.

Range Hood

Ventilation must be considered, especially if your kitchen is attached to the house or is under some sort of shelter. Range hoods, also known as vent hoods, remove the smoke and grease cooking generates, making the kitchen cleaner, safer, and more comfortable. A range hood can be mounted to the wall or ceiling, depending on the configuration of your outdoor kitchen. It's important to get one that is big enough to capture the rising cooking vapors. The best models have heat sensors that automatically increase power if temperatures reach a certain level.

Lighting

Grilling at night? Be sure you have light. Your outdoor kitchen should be well lit, but if you need additional light near the grill, consider a stand-alone fixture with a rotating head or a light that can clamp onto the grill handle or a nearby object. On some high-end grills, halogen lights are built into the grill hood.

Grill Cover

Many manufactures provide a cover when you buy your grill. A good grill cover should be constructed of heavy-duty vinyl with a nylon lining to protect your grill from the elements. You don't want your cover getting blown off on a windy day, so get one with Velcro tabs, snap closures, zippers, or a drawstring to ensure a snug fit.

When it comes to outfitting your grill, remember that you don't need every accessory. It's okay to "rough it" a little outdoors and leave the perfectly prepared meals to inside dining. Instead of relying on a rotisserie, for example, have a guest tend to the chicken. Sometimes, the simplest solutions are the best.

Other Cooking Options

A grill isn't the only way to go when it comes to preparing meals in an outdoor kitchen. Sure, it's the best bet if you want cheeseburgers or chicken breasts, but perhaps you're interested in smoking a few racks of ribs. Or maybe you'd like to bake pepperoni pizzas with crunchy crusts. The adventurous souls may like to barbecue some picanha (a special cut of beef popular in Brazil). If any of these scenarios make your mouth water, you should think about the following cooking options:

Smokers

Tell some folks you are going to "barbecue" something on your grill and they'll give you a strange look. To many people, a true barbecue consists of slowly smoking meat at a low temperature. Grilling is cooking directly over a high heat, charring the meat's surface and sealing in the juices, while barbecuing refers to using an indirect, low heat for a longer period of time to smoke-cook the meat. If the latter interests you, you may want a smoker.

The main difference between a charcoal grill and a smoker is that a smoker keeps the fire away from the food. Water smokers, which are shaped like a bullet, include a heat source on the bottom, grilling racks on the top, and a pan of water in between, creating a type of indirect cooking. The water pan ensures that foods will stay moist even after hours of cooking. Wood chips rest atop a heat source—charcoal is the most popular—and flavor the food. A dry smoker is the more traditional of the two types of smokers. It has an offset firebox on one side and a cooking chamber on the other. Rather than using charcoal or gas, dry smokers burn small pieces of wood in the firebox. A vent on the side opposite the firebox draws heat and smoke from the fire across the cooking chamber. The cooking chamber fills with smoke, giving the food its characteristic smoked flavor. Cooking times for a dry smoker tend to be longer than those for a water smoker because the food is farther from the heat source.

Kamados

The egg-shaped Kamado, a thick-walled ceramic cooker, is great for smoking at lower temperatures—between 150 and 250 degrees F—for long periods of time using only a small amount of charcoal. The ceramic walls retain the heat, and vents at the top and bottom allow you to control the temperature. Cooking space is limited; the largest models have a diameter of about 24 inches. Get one as large as possible because the long cooking times essentially make preparing everything at once a must.

Pizza Ovens

For the ultimate outdoor dining experience, many people are putting in a wood-fired pizza oven. These ovens, which reach temperatures unattainable in an indoor oven—600 to 700 degrees F is common—produce intense, even heat, resulting in pizzas with crisp crusts and sizzling toppings. It takes an hour or two for the oven to reach the required temperature, but the pizza cooks in a matter of minutes. The ovens can also be used for baking breads, roasting vegetables, and cooking meat.

Pizza oven kits, which cost about $2,000, are designed to be easy to install. Generally, the kit is housed in a

A dry smoker, left, contains the fire and keeps the temperature low. Cooking low and slow produces tender pieces of meat that practically fall off the bone.

The centerpiece of many new outdoor kitchens is a wood-fired pizza oven. This refractory concrete pizza oven, right, is heavy, so it requires a concrete footing.

masonry structure that can safely contain the high level of heat. The insert may be made of porous clay or concrete combined with firebricks, and the structure is usually covered with stucco, stone, or tile.

Adobe Ovens

An adobe oven is a low-tech alternative to a pizza oven that will keep more cash in your wallet. The basic adobe oven is simply an enclosure made of hardened mud, with a deep, arch-shaped opening in the front and a vent hole in the back. Many adobe ovens are sculpted works of art that look like something out of *Star Wars*. Adobe ovens, popular in the Southwest United States and Mexico, are not very heavy and do not require concrete footings, but they should rest on a fire-safe surface.

Churrasco Barbecues

A *churrascaria* is a Brazilian or Portuguese restaurant where large quantities of meat are prepared in a barbecue with a rotisserie that supports two or more levels of spits. This style of cooking is referred to as churrasco. Waiters go around with various cuts of meat on a skewer and slice off the pieces you request. Now, you can create these same pieces in your outdoor kitchen. A churrasco barbecue cooks meat using wood charcoal or firewood. It is different from a charcoal grill with a rotisserie because heat radiates from its oven-like walls, which helps seal in the juices and produce tender, juicy cuts of meat. If you're an expert mason, you may be able to build your own. For the rest of us, kits with stackable components are available, which makes adding a churrasco barbecue to your outdoor kitchen a lot more feasible.

The firebox portion of this churrasco barbecue is the perfect place to cook chicken, beef, and sausage on spits.

Churrasco Anatomy

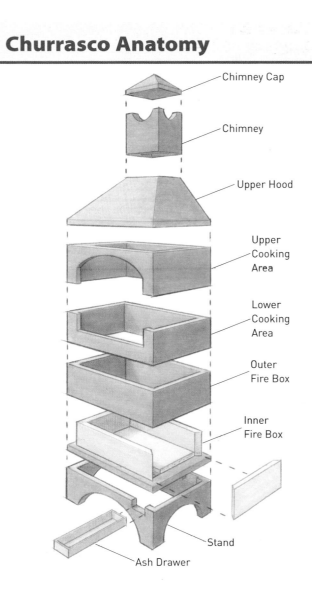

Chimney Cap

Chimney

Upper Hood

Upper Cooking Area

Lower Cooking Area

Outer Fire Box

Inner Fire Box

Stand

Ash Drawer

The 24-in. fridge holds the drinks, and the 15-in. ice machine provides a steady supply of ice cubes.

Refrigerators

You've got the meat. What about the cheese, the condiments, and the drinks? It doesn't make much sense to cook outdoors if you have to keep running back in the house for items. Add a refrigerator and your outdoor cooking area nearly becomes a fully functioning kitchen.

Under-counter refrigerators are the choice for most outdoor kitchens because they're out of sight, they're protected from the elements, and they allow counter space above. A full-size refrigerator should only be considered in a large, fully protected kitchen in a warm climate. Many manufacturers now make refrigerators for outdoor use. You will pay more money, but you'll get a fridge that typically has a larger compressor to keep your food cold and includes wiring and electronics designed to withstand the elements. The best ones are made of stainless steel, which stands up to the most extreme environments. Make sure your refrigerator has heavy door hinges that create a good door seal. It should also be front-vented so it can be placed under a countertop.

If you last purchased a compact fridge back when you were an undergrad living in a cramped dorm, be prepared to spend a bit more money this time. Most outdoor kitchen refrigerators start at $1,500, and a 24-inch stainless-steel model could set you back more than $2,000. Of course, you could always go low tech and just fill a cooler with ice and drinks and haul it outside. Put it on a stand or low shelf for convenience.

Smart Tip Save Energy

To reduce the amount of energy your refrigerator uses, keep it out of direct sunlight and position it away from the grill or any other heat source.

Other Outdoor Appliances

If you want your outdoor kitchen to be as efficient as its indoor counterpart, it makes sense to include some amenities. Small appliances are as indispensable outside as they are inside. Be sure that any appliance you will use outdoors is manufactured for that purpose. Whenever possible, look for items with the UL (Underwriters Laboratories Inc.) seal of approval.

Warming Drawer

A warming drawer that has a thermostatic temperature control will keep finished food items warm until dinner is served. The variable moisture control will help maintain the proper food texture, whether it's moist or crisp or somewhere in between. You'll often need to keep a lot of items—everything from bread to beets to beef—warm at the same time, so look for a unit with deep drawers.

Ice Maker

An ice maker, a slim appliance that can fit into a tight under-the-counter spot, will require a water line. Some models may also require a drain. If you're going to entertain often, look for a model that makes a large amount—25 to 35 pounds—in a short amount of time. Compact ice maker-refrigerator combos also are available.

Wine Cooler

What complements a fine meal better than a nice glass of wine? A wine cooler with an adjustable thermostat keeps your bottles at the perfect temperatures. Many wine coolers include automatic settings for red or white wine. Buy a wine cooler with a

security lock if you're worried about anyone raiding your collection. The smallest units hold 12 to 24 bottles; the next in line accommodate 28 to 32. The best come with canted shelves to keep corks moist.

Beer-Keg Dispenser

This is perhaps the final touch to your outdoor kitchen. A typical dispenser for the outdoor kitchen holds half kegs and quarter kegs. What better way to keep beer cold, fresh, and ready to serve? Some models include shelves that allow you to convert the dispenser into a fridge.

Let's not forget about the simple plug-in appliances. As long as you keep them sheltered, you can equip your outdoor kitchen with a blender, coffeemaker, toaster oven, waffle maker, juicer, and whatever else you may need. With so much available to outfit your outdoor kitchen, the only limitation is your imagination. Visit a few of the Web sites listed in the back of this book to check out some of the latest appliances.

Smart Tip **Plug It In**

Don't underestimate how many receptacles you will need. The gas grill will require an outlet, as will a side burner, a rotisserie, a refrigerator, a coffeemaker, and so on.

6

SELECTING APPLIANCES

A dispenser that holds a half-barrel keg keeps the beer cold and saves valuable refrigerator space.

CHAPTER 7

Easy Meal Preparation

SINKS AND COUNTERTOPS

C edar-planked salmon? Venison steak with Madeira sauce? Grilled vegetable pasta? Whatever recipes you've got in mind, adequate counter space will make your culinary adventures go smoothly. Trust us. You'll need room to prepare and serve your food, and room to clean up the mess afterward. Built-in side shelves of a typical freestanding grill just won't do the trick.

In the not so distant past, the deck's patio table served as the operations center. No longer. Today's outdoor kitchen features durable, beautiful countertops in a wide range of materials, from ceramic tile to natural stone.

To complete the picture, consider installing a sink and running water as well. While not a necessity, it will provide a place to rinse fruits and vegetables, fill pots, and wash dishes. And as with countertops, the array of sinks—and faucets—is vast.

Don't forget that all that cooking—sink or no sink—will create a fair share of garbage. Remember to include a trash container in your outdoor kitchen, and consider how you'll handle recycling and composting, too.

A large sink has its benefits in an outdoor kitchen. This single-bowl sink is best for washing large items, such as roasting pans, grilling utensils, and deep pots.

Countertops

One of the first things a person notices when entering a kitchen is the countertop. It's a prominent element that helps define the room and set its personality. But while good looks are important, consider function, too. The material you choose must be durable enough to stand up to hot pans, chopping, and spills of all sorts. It should also be easy to clean and sanitize. Generally, the less porous the counter, the better it will be. It also must contend with the heat, cold, and moisture that mother nature doles out, especially if your kitchen is uncovered.

Materials

No countertop material is perfect for everything. Each has its pluses and minuses. The factors you deem most important, combined with the look you prefer, will ultimately determine the material that is best for your outdoor kitchen. Some popular choices follow.

Stone If you want your outdoor kitchen to withstand abuse from the elements, a stone countertop is a natural choice. Stone, whether it's granite, marble, soapstone, or limestone, is durable and beautiful. It does, however, require periodic treatment, and it's difficult to repair should you somehow manage to damage it.

The most popular natural stone choice for countertops is granite, a durable surface that's resistant to chips, scratches, and stains. It's impervious to high temperatures, so feel free to set down that hot pot. Granite is quarried naturally, so every piece is unique. It is somewhat porous, so the countertop will require sealing at least once a year. Your granite countertop can be dressed to a honed or polished finish. Avoid a matte finish because it's more susceptible to staining. Clean up spills with warm water and a soft cloth. Granite's drawbacks? It's heavy, so it requires sturdy support. And it's expensive. The cost depends on many factors, including color, finish, size, and origin.

Want to impress the neighbors? Go with marble. The

classic colors and beautiful veining make for a gorgeous surface. However, marble is more porous than granite and requires more maintenance if you want to keep it looking its best. It will need to be sealed about once a year. If left unfinished, it stains easily, and acids, such as vinegar, will etch it. Because it does come with a hefty price tag—and because there is a risk of chipping it—consider using marble sparingly in prominent locations and filling the remaining area with less-expensive options.

You may recognize soapstone, with its dark-gray color and honed appearance, from your high school science classroom. It's a durable material that is less expensive than granite but softer, too, necessitating greater care. Treat soapstone with mineral oil to protect it from stains. Soapstone may not be as resilient as granite, but it is resistant to heat, so hot pots and pans won't damage it.

Softer still is limestone. Because of its high porosity, limestone needs to be sealed more often than other natural stones—at least once a year—to reduce staining. If you choose this material, be prepared to provide plenty of TLC.

Tile Ceramic tile, another popular choice for an outdoor kitchen countertop, is easy to install and allows for plenty of creative designs. It's available in a wide range of sizes, styles, colors, and patterns. If you decide to go with ceramic tile, be sure to use tile rated for use on countertops. Your best bet for outdoor use are tiles rated as "impervious." These tiles, which are fired in the kiln the longest at the highest temperatures, allow almost no water absorption and are resistant to heat, cold, stains, and scratches. Ceramic tile is either glazed or unglazed. Glazed tiles are preferable for your outdoor countertop because they are more stain resistant and are easier to clean. Another alternative is porcelain tile, which is fired at a much higher temperature than regular ceramic tile. This makes porcelain tile much harder and denser than other tiles. Tile can crack or chip if you drop a pot on it, but what turns off many homeowners more are the grout lines, which tend to stain and host bacteria—especially outdoors, where surfaces stay damp longer and people don't clean up as quickly outside as they do inside. If you do opt for a tile counter, use a nonstaining epoxy grout.

Concrete Concrete is made by mixing portland cement, sand, and gravel with water. For more info on concrete, which is becoming increasingly popular as a countertop material, see "Pros and Cons of Concrete Countertops" on page 126.

Soapstone countertops, opposite, are a popular choice for an outdoor kitchen. They will last a long time—if you remember to treat them periodically.

Solid-surface countertops, right, can be considered if your kitchen is under a roof. This countertop is adequately protected from harmful UV rays.

Sealing the Deal

When selecting a sealer for your concrete countertop, look for one that offers resistance to stains (red wine, lemon juice, olive oil) and heat, requires infrequent sealing, and is EPA and FDA compliant for contact with food.

The curve in this beautiful granite countertop, above, fits better with the landscape and makes the cooking area more compact.

The shelf, right, which is also made from granite, is a space-saving way to add to your countertop.

A stainless-steel countertop is a seamless way to tie together stainless-steel appliances and cabinets in your outdoor kitchen. It's pricey, but it will last.

Stainless Steel   Stainless steel, a durable material with a sleek look, is getting more popular in residential settings. It is sanitary, waterproof, and stainproof, but it can scratch, so use a cutting board. It's never affected by heat, so hot pots are not a problem unless you drop one—which may result in a dent that will be difficult to repair. Fingerprints may also find their way onto your stainless-steel countertop, but those are much easier to eliminate. Glass cleaner will do the trick. Wash your stainless-steel countertop with warm water and a cloth. Dry it with a towel or cloth, wiping in the direction of the metal's polish lines.

Be Cautious about These Materials   Be cautious about using certain traditional countertop materials in an outdoor kitchen. These include solid-surfacing material and engineered stone (also known as *quartz composite*). Solid-surfacing material is made from polymer blends. Engineered stone, although comprised mostly of quartz, includes polymer resin binders. Polymers are susceptible to damage from UV light, so many manufacturers will not warrant solid-surfacing material for outdoor use. Otherwise, this material makes an excellent countertop. It is stain resistant, has few or no seams in which bacteria can hide, and is easy to maintain, requiring no sealing. Con-sider using solid-surfacing material on your counter if your outdoor kitchen includes a roof.

Wood countertops also pose problems when used outdoors, especially in environments that are frequently damp. They are relatively difficult to keep clean, and they don't hold up well to sun exposure or wet, cold weather. Wood is also prone to heat and water damage, so it's likely to warp or rot if installed anywhere near a water or heat source. Once again, use only if protected from sun and rain, and if proper clearances are observed.

Laminate countertops, while a great value for an indoor kitchen, aren't meant for the great outdoors. Moisture can build up in the base material, causing the laminate to expand and buckle. Big swings in temperature can do the same thing.

Smart Tip Before You Buy

When choosing a countertop surface, go directly to the fabricator after you have an idea of what you'd like. Look at the largest samples available. Small sample chips can be misleading.

Pros and Cons of Concrete Countertops

Looking for a countertop material that's a good substitute for stone and offers an outlet for creativity? Look no further than concrete. It's a lot more interesting than the drab, gray material that people associate with sidewalks and basement floors. In fact, a concrete countertop can be stunning. Depending how it's treated, it can be made to appear slick and shiny or rough and textured. Leave it looking natural and it can complement the wood, stone, or brick on your home or in your yard. Concrete looks great outdoors and works with many styles, from Colonial to Southwestern.

Using concrete for your countertop gives you the most design freedom. You can choose the shapes—including curves and angles—the colors, and even the inlays. If you really want to personalize your outdoor kitchen's countertop, you can embed seashells, glass chips, coins, broken dishware, and other personal mementos.

Concrete countertops are sometimes poured, or cast, in place, or they can be prefabricated and delivered to the job site. Most are precast in molds built to the customer's specs so they can be formed, cured, and finished under controlled conditions. Casting in place, which involves building forms and poring the concrete directly on the cabinets, avoids the hassles of transporting heavy slabs, but it does tie up the site for days—or weeks. Precast concrete countertops move all the processes off site, providing more quality control over the finished product.

Because each concrete countertop is a custom job, it's sometimes more costly than other options. And the price only goes up when you incorporate edgings, inlays, sinks, curved backsplashes, and other complex details.

Another drawback? Bare concrete is very porous, so almost all concrete countertops are sealed and then waxed to prevent stains. To maintain appearance and function, the countertop needs to be sealed about once a year and waxed at least three or four times annually.

Concrete is a durable, scratch-resistant material, but the sealer can scratch. Cutting on the concrete may compromise the integrity of the sealer, so use a cutting board when slicing tomatoes for the burgers. The sealer is also susceptible to damage and discoloration from heat, so consider installing a trivet directly on the countertop (and close to the grill). That way, you can place a hot pot on it and not worry about affecting the sealer.

Don't forget that concrete, available in slabs up to 10 feet long, is heavy—very heavy. Concrete countertops may need more support than the base cabinets below. But if you can create a foundation that can buttress this one-of-a-kind surface that expresses style and individuality, concrete is hard to beat.

Stone tile was used for this curved outdoor kitchen countertop. Its colors and shine go well with the kitchen's stucco finish.

A concrete countertop, above, is a completely customized product, so it may take four to six weeks to fabricate.

Ceramic tile was used to top this two-tiered counter, left, which is great for preparing meals and dining.

Edges

When it comes to selecting a countertop edge, the primary factor should be appearance. You'll have to live with it, so you might as well love it. Just keep in mind that any crease in the edge profile is a potential trap for food and dirt. The more elaborate the countertop edge, the more maintenance it will require.

A *straight edge* is standard. It is squared, with a very slight bevel to remove the sharpness from the top and bottom edges. A popular alternative is the *quarter round*, with a rounded-off top edge. Another variation is the *bullnose;* the top and bottom edges are rounded more dramatically, giving it the appearance of a bullet when viewed in profile. *Beveled* edges are also popular, and the bevel can be carved at quarter length or half length. More decorative edges, such as the *ogee* (concave and convex lines that resemble an S), will bump up the price. The availability of these fancier edges varies based on the countertop material selected.

Counter Space

You know what kind of countertop you want. You've even chosen the perfect countertop edge. Now, it's time to figure out just how much counter space you're going to need to make your outdoor kitchen fully functional.

Indoors or out, ample counter space is a must. You need room to prepare food, to serve meals, and to hold a variety of items. Nobody wants to fumble with hot pots and pans while searching for a place to lay them down. Don't skimp. Plan on having 36 inches of work space on each side of the grill. If your kitchen includes a sink, make food prep and cleanup easier by allowing 18 to 24 inches of open space on both sides of it. A 4-foot-long counter is ideal for serving, and if people will be eating at the counter, make sure you provide about 24 inches in width per person.

Countertop Dimensions

A comfortable counter height for most adults is 36 inches. The counter should be 32 to 36 inches high, but consider having it customized if the primary cook is very tall or very short. A typical bar counter will be a tad higher, usually 42 to 46 inches high. Or go with a tiered design. Use the lower surface for slicing cheese and chopping vegetables, and serve drinks on the higher surface. Tiered designs also screen the prep area from a formal dining area. The countertop should be at least 24 inches deep, with more depth (at least 42 inches) necessary if the counter will be accessible from both sides.

Countertop Edge Profiles

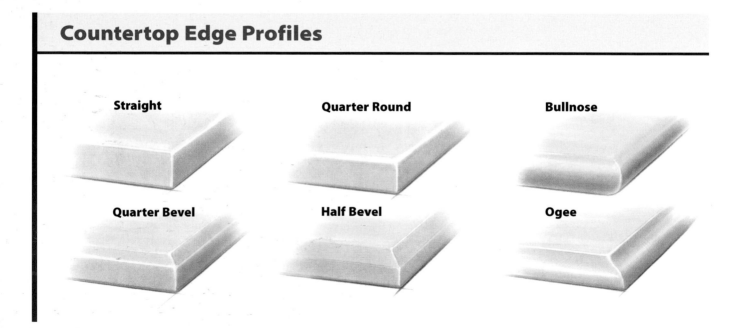

Straight

Quarter Round

Bullnose

Quarter Bevel

Half Bevel

Ogee

The bullnose edging of this countertop, above, matches the bullnose edging of the sill above it.

Consider style when selecting a countertop edge. A straight (squared) edge looks good here, right, because it plays off the uneven surface of the stone facing nicely.

Smart Tip Finding Space

Outdoor countertops are typically smaller than their indoor counterparts. Conserve space by eliminating unnecessary items and by keeping necessities on nearby shelves and hooks.

Sinks

Some people include "everything but the kitchen sink" in their outdoor kitchen. They choose to do without a sink, content to make do with a grill, some storage, and counter space. Is a sink necessary in your outdoor kitchen? It does make life easier by providing easy, immediate cleanup, though that might not be much of a problem if your outdoor kitchen is close to the house. The farther from the house, the more indispensable a sink becomes—the more difficult and costly to install, too.

Unless you're okay with a simple hose-feed, a sink requires an underground water supply and drain lines. The lines often run in deep trenches and for long distances, so it's best to have a professional dig the trenches, run the lines, and make the hookups to the house. This, of course, adds to the cost of your outdoor kitchen. The sink drain will probably need to be connected to the house's drain system, though codes may allow you to discharge the sink to a dry well, which can be as simple as a small pit filled with gravel. A dry well slowly disperses drain water into the surrounding earth, which is okay as long as you use biodegradable detergents. For hot water, of course, you'll need a second supply line. This will boost your installation and energy costs but will make dishwashing a lot nicer. You could always save money by using your grill's side burner to heat water for dishwashing purposes.

A small, round sink works best in outdoor kitchens where space is tight. This sink comes in handy when it's time to clean grilling utensils or wash herbs.

Smart Tip Waterworks

If you live in an area with freezing temperatures, water connections should be buried below the frost line and insulated. It's also important to install valves so you can shut off the water from inside the house and drain any water that's trapped in the line.

Self-rimming sinks are the most common style of sink. They are almost always the least expensive, too.

Sink Selection

Choosing an outdoor sink is not much different from choosing an indoor one. In fact, manufacturers have not yet come up with a product specifically designated for outdoor use. If you visit a showroom, many salesmen will simply point to a stainless-steel bar sink and tell you it's what most people install. Nevertheless, select a sink that meets your needs. If you want to wash dishes in it, you'll want something a lot bigger than a bar sink. But if you're only going to use it to rinse off fruit and veggies, you can get by with something small.

Styles Sinks come in five basic styles: drop-in, under-mount, integral, vessel, and apron.

Drop-in, or self-rimming, sinks are by far the most common. They provide the easiest installation and are the least expensive. The major drawback? The rim stands $1/8$ to $1/4$ inch above the counter surface, creating a place for food crumbs, dirt, and bacteria to collect.

Under-mount sinks, which are attached to the under-side of the counter, have no exposed rims or edges to capture dirt, water, and germs. They are ideally suited for outdoor kitchens, especially those with stone, concrete, or solid-surface countertops.

Integral sinks call for careful planning. You will have to know exactly where the sink will go before ordering the countertop. Integral sinks are made of the same material as the counter—typically stone, concrete, stainless steel, or solid surfacing material. Integral sinks are installed flush with the counter surface, so you can sweep crumbs and scraps off the counter directly into the sink.

Apron sinks are typically large, rectangular, and deep. They're installed in the same fashion as under-mounts but left exposed to display the front of the sink, which is often decoratively treated. To install an apron sink, you must plan on a stone, concrete, or solid-surface countertop.

Vessel sinks, which sit atop the counter, have been a hot trend in bathrooms and are finding their way into kitchens. They make a major design statement. But they are entirely exposed to the elements, so think twice before installing one outdoors.

This under-mount sink with an apron front is made of durable fireclay. It's reminiscent of a turn-of-the-century farmhouse sink.

Few vessel sinks have predrilled holes for faucets, so you'll need a place to mount the faucet—usually the wall behind the counter. This copper sink doubles as a piece of art.

Things to Consider   In an outdoor kitchen, a *single-bowl* sink is best for doing a lot of washing by hand. Having a *double-bowl* sink would let you multitask—fill a pot in one bowl; rinse dishes in the other—or allow you to have two people working at the same time, which is nice, but it's probably not necessary outdoors. In addition, the divider may get in the way when you try to wash a large pot or platter.

Most sinks are square or rectangular, but other options are available. A *round* sink might work best where space is at a premium, especially if it's to be installed in a corner. The sink can also be *oval* or *quarter-round*. A *trough* sink, which is longer and leaner than its traditional counterparts is popular. The extra elbow room allows more than one person to work at the sink at the same time, and it provides a great place to serve drinks or shrimp on ice.

Although a single-bowl sink should suffice in an outdoor kitchen, make sure it's large enough to hold a meal's worth of dishes. A *prep sink*—a small sink that assists with food preparation and cleanup—may be too small. If you've got the room, go with a sink that's large enough to rinse your pots, pans, and grill grates. Depth is an important consideration, too. The typical sink is about 8 inches deep. For filling (and rinsing) large pots and pans, you may want one that is 10 or 12 inches deep.

If you mount your sink under the counter, you'll have no crevices for crumbs. This under-mount model has a single basin that is 7½ in. deep.

Sink Materials

Stainless-steel sinks are preferable for your outdoor sink, and with good reason. They hold up to the elements and will not corrode. Stainless steel is lightweight, easy to install, and easy to clean. It's resistant to heat and stains, and it won't chip or crack, but it can dent and show scratches. And it can be noisy, though some sink manufacturers have introduced models with sound-deadening technologies to reduce noise. Stainless steel is measured by its thickness, and in general, the thicker the steel—the lower the gauge—the quieter the sink will be. An 18-gauge stainless-steel sink is recommended.

If you're looking for a brightly colored sink, *enameled steel* is an economical option. It's not sensitive to heat, but chipping can occur. *Enameled cast iron*, which used to be the sink standard, is okay, too. It's a durable material that's resistant to scratches and chips. But its durability comes with a price; enameled cast iron is more expensive than stainless steel or enameled steel. It's heavy, too, so you must have a cabinet that can accommodate the weight.

A *fireclay* sink can withstand high temperatures and resists stains and scratches. It offers a smooth surface that won't rust, fade, or discolor. It's easy to clean, too. But fireclay, popular with apron sinks, is a costly option.

Composite stone sinks are a mix of stone and acrylic. These durable sinks don't stain or scratch easily, and they are resistant to heat, so a hot pot can go straight from the grill to the sink without leaving a mark.

Solid-surface sinks are popular because, like composite sinks, they can be integrated right into the countertop. This makes for a clean, seamless surface. A solid-surface sink won't stain and is easy to clean, but it's softer than a composite-stone sink and can get nicked, scratched, and dented. It won't hold up as well to hot pots, either. It's more expensive than most other options, as well.

If your outdoor sink won't be subject to lots of wear and tear, you could consider a decorative but lighter-duty copper or brass sink.

Cheaper Alternatives

If you'd love an outdoor sink but don't relish the thought of digging trenches, laying pipes, and making connections to the house, consider hooking the garden hose to the sink. Remember to disconnect and stow the hose before the temperatures drop below freezing. For drainage, consider a portable gray-water reservoir. A 5- to 15-gallon plastic tub under the sink might do the trick.

Portable units hooked up to a garden hose are also available for those who don't want to install a sink into the countertop. For less than $1,000, you can have a single- or double-bowl sink at your disposal whenever you need to wash your hands or clean your cooking utensils.

Smart Tip **The Hole Story**

When purchasing a sink, keep in mind how many holes will be needed for the faucet and other accessories (side sprayer, soap dispenser, and so forth). Stainless-steel and porcelain enamel sinks must be ordered with the proper drillings.

The basin of this vessel sink, made from natural rock, was hand-ground and polished. Vessel sinks aren't too deep. The depth of this model is only 3¼ in.

A built-in sink is not a must in an outdoor kitchen. This single-basin utility sink, right, with a two-hole faucet drilled into an integrated backsplash sits in a wood stand. The cast-iron sink, which holds more than 16 gallons, can be disconnected and stored away when not needed.

Stainless steel is the most popular choice for an outdoor sink. The curved design of this self-rimming model, left, accommodates the natural motion of the arms.

A soapstone sink with a dark charcoal color gives an outdoor kitchen a rustic look—and it requires very little maintenance. This single-bowl sink, right, is 7³/₄ in. deep.

Faucets

Your first priority will be to find a faucet that's going to be easy to use, but you shouldn't have to give up on style. Virtually any faucet made for indoor kitchens can be used outdoors, so you'll have plenty from which to choose. Costs range from as little as $50 to $300 and up for a top-quality unit. Choose the latter if you're going to be cooking outdoors frequently. Whatever you pay, be sure to inquire about the ease of getting replacement parts, and look for a faucet that comes with a lifetime warranty against leaks, drips, and finish defects.

Types

A *pull-down spray*—a faucet with a spout that pulls out to become a sprayer—is popular. The pull-down spray makes it easy to wash vegetables, rinse pasta, and clean dirty dishes. Another outdoor favorite is the *gooseneck* faucet, and with good reason. The gooseneck design—a curved, U-shaped spout with a high arc—allows for easy filling of large pots. *Pot-fillers* are also becoming popular. A restaurant-style pot-filler, which is a spout on a hinged arm, can be mounted in the counter or on the wall—on a backsplash, perhaps. A pot-filler easily swivels and allows you to fill a pot with ease.

This faucet, left, has it all. The gooseneck design allows for easy filling of big pots. The spout pulls out, making it easy to wash veggies and clean dishes. The single handle operates easier than its dual-handled counterparts.

Need to wash your fruits and vegetables? This faucet with a pullout spout, opposite, makes that task a lot simpler. The spout is attached to a 59-in. braided hose, offering plenty of reach. The spout swings when not pulled out.

Smart Tip Purified Water

Tired of buying bottled water? Water filters can be incorporated directly into the faucet. Filtering faucets start at around $300 and are usually housed under the sink; others are situated inside the spout.

Handles

Single-handled faucets have an edge when it comes to outdoor kitchens. They're easier to operate and take up less space than dual-handled faucets. They also avoid the confusion that might result from having a dual-handled faucet in which only the cold-water side is operational. If you do have hot and cold water, single-handled faucets take only one hand to use, freeing the other to hold a pot or a spatula. A lever or knob controls both hot and cold. You can also go with separate handles for hot and cold water—the most common indoor setup. This "widespread faucet" takes up more room because it requires separate holes for hot water, cold water, and the spout, but it allows you to adjust water temperature more precisely.

Valves

Every faucet has an inner valve that controls water flow through the spout. The valve is the heart of the faucet. Select one that is dependable and prevents the dreaded drip. Four types of valves are available: compression, cartridge (or washerless), ball, and ceramic disc. Compression faucets, which always have two controls, are the least reliable. Most of today's faucets feature a cartridge, ball, or ceramic-disc valve. The most durable, reliable choice is the ceramic-disc faucet, which offers precise control and is nearly maintenance free. It's also the most expensive.

Other Options

A side sprayer—a small spray nozzle connected to a pull-out hose—increases function and flexibility when hosing down dishes or cleaning the inside of the sink. A spout that swings from side to side allows for greater reach and versatility. For those who want to conserve energy, an aerator is a must. Aerators inject air into the water to reduce the flow rate while maintaining pressure. These water-saving devices enable you to adjust the flow of water; you can immediately switch from a steady stream (for rinsing those dirty dishes) to a soft spray (for washing vegetables).

Finishes

While any good faucet will work outdoors, it may need to be replaced or repaired a few years sooner than one on an indoor sink. A stainless-steel faucet will handle the outdoor elements and is easy to maintain. A solid-brass faucet (available with a variety of finishes) is another particularly durable option. When polished, a metal faucet provides a contemporary look and does a good job at hiding scratches. A brushed-metal finish has a more old-fashioned feel and does a better job of hiding water spots and fingerprints than a polished faucet. It seems more at home in a garden setting as well. Today's better faucets, regardless of finish, have special coatings that resist scratches and abrasive cleaners.

A lever, opposite, can be operated with one hand, making it easy to clean freshly caught fish.

This single-control faucet, above, with a polished-chrome finish, has ceramic-disc valves.

Chrome may be easier to maintain, but some people prefer the look of antique bronze, right.

Trash

Having a sink in your outdoor kitchen is optional, but including a trash container is essential. Outdoor trash receptacles come in all shapes, sizes, and materials. Most are stainless steel, which holds up well outdoors. If your container will be kept out in the open, consider one with a foot pedal, so your hands don't have to touch the bin. It's more sanitary, and it comes in handy when you've got your hands filled with trash. Looking for a high-tech refuse resolution? Try a pail with a lid that opens and closes automatically using infrared technology and a smart chip. For a good low-tech solution, install a hook near your trash station where you can hang the lid while using the container.

In many outdoor kitchens, the garbage pail is kept out of sight, either under the sink or in a cabinet of its own. The latter seems to be the most popular solution. These pails are either tilted out or pulled out on full-extension slides. Some of them have a lid that lifts when the cabinet door is opened. An innovative way to keep your trash out of

Pullout trash cabinets are popular. Pull them out only when you need them, and keep containers out of sight.

Stainless-steel outdoor cabinets made specifically for trash are available. This 18-in.-wide model includes full-extension slides. The toe kick is optional.

A top-mounted container installed in a cabinet near where the most trash is generated makes it easily accessible at the most crucial moments.

sight, especially if you have a small floor area, is to mount the lid over an opening in the counter. The waste receptacle sits inside the cabinet.

No matter where your garbage pail winds up in your outdoor kitchen, be vigilant about emptying it frequently. If not, don't be surprised if you have squirrels, raccoons, and other unwelcome guests. Remove the trash after each meal and put it in a sealed garbage can.

Recycling

You may choose to devote space in your outdoor kitchen to day-to-day recycling needs. A pullout pail under the cabinet works well, as does a freestanding container that can be toted to the garage and emptied into your primary recycling bin when full. Corner base cabinets and under-the-sink areas offer less than ideal storage for regular items, so they make good locations for recyclables as well.

A teak receptacle with pyramid-shaped corner posts is an elegant way to hide trash or recyclables.

Composting

Reduce trash volume and produce mounds of plant-nourishing compost by putting your organic kitchen waste into a composter. Collect scraps in a small lidded bucket placed near your sink; then transfer the scraps to your composter. You can compost almost anything that is organic, including fruit and vegetable scraps, coffee grounds, tea bags, eggshells, grass clippings, animal hair, and small amounts of shredded paper and soft cardboard. Do not put meat, cheese, or fish in your compost bin.

Smart Tip Sunbathe Your Bin

Place your compost bin in a sunny spot on well-drained soil, preferably somewhere discreet.

In or Out?

What to Compost	
Animal manure	Wood chips
Cardboard rolls	Wool rags
Clean paper	Yard trimmings
Coffee filters	
Coffee grounds	**What Not**
Cotton rags	**to Compost**
Dryer and vacuum-cleaner	Black walnut-tree leaves
lint	or twigs
Eggshells	Coal or charcoal ash
Fireplace ashes	Dairy products (butter,
Fruits and vegetables	egg yolks, sour cream,
Grass clippings	yogurt, and so forth)
Hair and fur	Diseased or insect-ridden
Hay and straw	plants
Houseplants	Fats, grease, lard, or oils
Leaves	Meat or fish bones and
Nutshells	scraps
Sawdust	Pet wastes (feces, soiled
Shredded newspaper	cat litter, and so forth)
Tea bags	Yard trimmings treated
	with pesticides

Note: If you are fertilizing fruits or vegetables with your compost, stick to items that you know are free of chemicals.

ELECTRONIC
IGNITION

CHAPTER 8

Organize Your Kitchen

STORAGE OPTIONS

Spending thousands of dollars on an outdoor kitchen doesn't make much sense if it's going to be too cluttered to work comfortably. Carefully planned storage, even in a small space, can make all the difference. Most storage plans begin with the grill, either by building the grill into a counter (often called an island) or by flanking a freestanding grill with counters. Grill counters can be built of a variety of materials. Typically, however, masonry is used—especially if the kitchen is exposed to the elements. Masonry also tends to blend better with the landscape. Grill counters can be custom-built or prefabricated.

There is no need to limit your storage to a grill counter. More elaborate outdoor kitchens have long runs of masonry counters that accommodate doors and drawers as well as sinks and other appliances. They can be designed in any shape, from L to S. Openings in the masonry can accommodate everything from drawers and doors to electrical receptacles and built-in lights. Storage, however, needn't be limited to what you can build from masonry. Today's outdoor kitchens are often outfitted with base cabinets and wall cabinets made from stainless steel, plastic, and wood. In addition, drawers, shelves, racks, hooks, countertops, and carts can all work together to provide a place for everything you need.

A fully functioning outdoor kitchen should include storage devices of all kinds. These stainless-steel drawers are perfect for utensils and all of your favorite spices.

Custom Versus Prefab

Outdoor kitchen counters can be custom-built or assembled from prefabricated components. The former are permanent structures built of masonry, metal, or wood. You can choose materials that blend well with your home's surroundings. Think carefully, however, about spending big bucks on something you can't take with you should you move.

That's where prefabricated counters, which can be modified to meet your specifications, come into play. Prefab units cost less than custom counters, require no building permits, and can go with you if you move. It's for those reasons, and others, that prefab kitchens are becoming more popular.

Custom Counters

Most outdoor kitchen counters are custom-built, sometimes after a landscape architect or a kitchen designer helps create one that matches your specific desires. The counters are then permanently installed—probably with the assistance of a contractor. Custom counters allow much more design flexibility than prefabricated models can offer. They do require more legwork (securing permits, laying a foundation, building the structure, and so on) and are more costly, but they add value to your home.

Custom counters are commonly made of concrete block. They can also be built with steel or wood framing, brick, or stone. When selecting a structural material, keep looks, cost, and labor in mind. Make a choice that fits in with the style of your home. Incorporate similar colors, textures, and styles for a uniform appearance. The counter's base, for example, can match the brick on your patio. The tiles used around your pool can be incorpo-rated into the countertop. Take a look at your surroundings—house, garage, patio, fencing, landscape—to get ideas about which of the following structural materials would work best for your outdoor kitchen.

Masonry

Many outdoor kitchens are made of concrete block, stone, or brick, and for good reason. Masonry materials are chosen for their appearance and their durability. Note, how-

A wood-fired oven, opposite top, was incorporated into this outdoor kitchen. The front wall is made of cast concrete, and the other walls will be built of concrete block.

The finished L-shape kitchen, opposite bottom, houses a grill, side burner, sink, and plenty of storage, in addition to the oven. The unit has a stucco finish.

Concrete block was used as the structure for this outdoor kitchen, below, which is finished with architectural stone.

ever, that this durable structure must sit on a solid foundation. In many cases, this means a steel-reinforced concrete slab that is thick enough—typically 4 to 6 inches—to satisfy local building codes.

Concrete Block Concrete block, also known as concrete masonry units, is a rugged, structurally sound material that is less expensive and more readily available than stone. It's noncombustible, too, which is key for any structure that will house a grill. Rough-face concrete block has an attractive stone-like texture. Or you can opt to cover block with a stone, brick, or stucco facing. For more information about facings, see the next page.

Stone Stones of various sizes, shapes, and colors work in any outdoor setting. They fit in with the landscape and contrast nicely with the stainless-steel accessories. Building with stone is a bit tricky, however, because of its weight and the irregular shapes. For stability, a stone wall is generally built thicker than a concrete block or brick wall. It's also more difficult to install built-in grills, appliances, and cabinets into a stone structure. For these reasons, many homeowners opt to build with a different material and clad it with a stone or manufactured-stone facing. This way, you get the look you want while avoiding

Granite counters and shelves extend from both sides of this brick cooking station, providing plenty of storage.

the construction problems stone presents.

Brick Brick fits into almost every outdoor setting and complements nearly every architectural style. Most people prefer the look of common brick, but it's porous, so it's less durable than firebrick, which is slightly larger and heavier—and more expensive. Be sure the bricks are graded for outdoor use. If you live in an area that has freezing temperatures, look for bricks graded "SX" by the Brick Institute of America.

Steel

Counters can also be framed with steel and covered with concrete backer board. Such units are strong, withstand freezing temperatures, and, like those built of concrete block, are fire resistant. Steel framing is lighter than concrete block. So

This lightweight counter with cypress doors can go on the deck or the patio without requiring a concrete footing.

much lighter, in fact, that a well-framed deck can support it. Steel framing—competitive in price with wood—is easier to install than masonry and allows for construction with straighter lines and tighter corners, which usually allows more cabinet space than a similarly sized masonry unit can provide.

Wood

Don't discount a wood-framed kitchen counter. After all, your deck, trellis, shed, and other outdoor structures are likely made of wood. A wood-framed structure is the easiest to build, and if offers plenty of design flexibility. It's one of the lightest structures, too, which means it won't need

a thick concrete footing. As long as the countertop is not made from concrete or another heavy material, your wood-framed counter will probably be light enough to rest on your deck. Wood's biggest downside is that it's flammable. Safety is a major issue. Be sure your grill has an insulating jacket, and check the grill manufacturer's recommendations to be sure the wood surfaces are protected from the heat of the grill.

Facings and Finishes

How does it look? Will it hold up? Those are the two key questions to keep in mind when selecting a facing for your custom kitchen counters. Concrete block or backer

Counter Anatomy

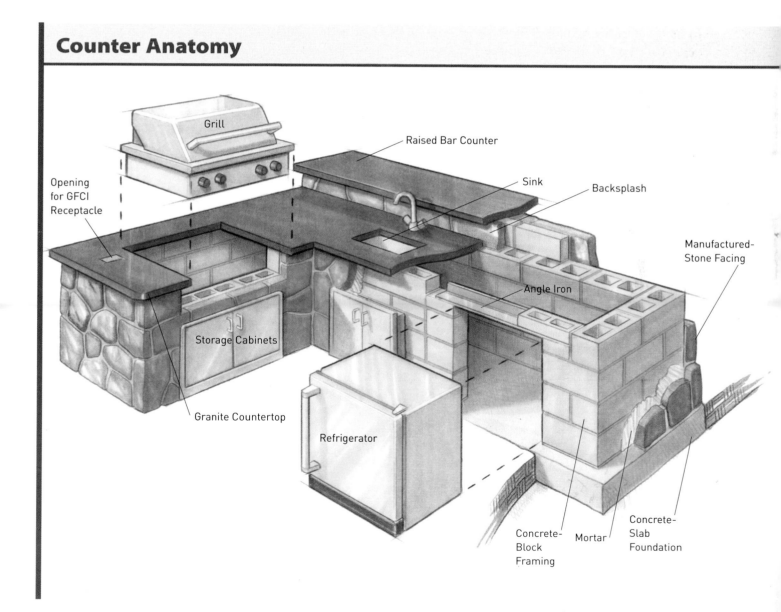

Smart Tip Thin Is In

Will you be facing your custom kitchen counters with natural stone? Keep labor issues in mind. The thinner and lighter the stone, the easier it will be to install.

board can be finished with any durable material. Here are the most common choices:

Tile If you'd like straight lines and a contemporary look, your best bet is tile facing. Glazed ceramic tile is the popular choice for a countertop, but stone tile is the typical choice for facing, although ceramic tile can be used. Natural-stone tiles cut into straight-sided pieces—usually about 12 inches per side—provide a natural feel. Possibilities include granite, marble, and slate. Stone tiles will be durable if you apply acrylic sealer every couple of years. Ceramic tiles come in a wide variety of colors, shapes, and textures. Impervious ceramic tiles are a wise choice for outdoor use; they are resistant to extreme temperatures, water, stains, and scratches. Tile, whether it's stone or ceramic, offers plenty of design options.

Natural Stone If you have stainless-steel doors and

A stone finish, above—whether it's natural stone or manufactured stone—complements stainless-steel appliances and looks great in almost any outdoor setting.

Common brick is a popular choice for outdoor kitchen counters, but it's not the only choice. Other face bricks, below, are available.

appliances, they will blend nicely with a natural-stone facing. Your outdoor kitchen will have a rugged, rustic look, whether you use random shapes and sizes for a jigsaw-puzzle appearance or go with squared-off pieces for a stone-wall look. Stone can be purchased at a stone yard or a brickyard. The thin stones that are suitable for covering a vertical surface may be called face stone or flagstone. Some stone, especially granite, is difficult to cut.

Manufactured Stone Manufactured stone, also called "engineered stone" or "faux stone," is cheaper than natural stone. For a long time, it didn't look like the real thing, but advances in technology have made it so that you might not even be able to tell the difference. Manufactured stone is made by pouring cement, pigment, and a lightweight filler such as pumice

Stuccoing a Wood-Frame Counter

Stucco is typically applied to concrete block or brick, but don't discount it if you're building with wood. When applying stucco over wood framing, first fasten an expanded metal lath to the wall sheathing with staples. The stucco protects the sheathing and interior of the counter from moisture damage. Three coats are necessary. The first layer, also referred to as the scratch coat, is applied ¼ to ½ inch thick using a mason's trowel. While the first coat is still a bit wet, scratch the surface with a comb-like tool—the ridges that are created help to hold the next layer—and then allow the first coat to cure for a couple of days, keeping it moist with an occasional spraying. The second coat, applied about ¼ inch thick, makes the stucco more durable. It should also cure for two days while being kept moist. The finish coat, also about ¼ inch thick, should be applied over a dampened second coat. Use stiff bristle brushes to impart texture or trowels to create a smooth finish. After it's textured to your liking, spray the surface with a fine mist; cover with plastic sheeting; and allow to cure for at least four days— longer if you want to paint the stucco. Some new stucco products are modified with polymers, curing agents, and reinforcing fibers to help control cracking in thinner applications. They are faster and easier to apply than traditional stucco.

into molds. The textures, shapes, and colors of real stone can be replicated with exacting detail. The appearance and cost (about half that of natural stone) are the main selling points, but because manufactured stone is lighter than natural stone, it's also easier to install. It usually doesn't require the poured footing that a natural-stone wall would. And because it's concrete, it stands up to harsh weather, whether it's a Florida downpour or Arizona's dry heat.

Brick To bring that cozy, traditional feel to the backyard, many people opt for a brick facing. Common brick, which blends well with many home styles, is popular, but other face bricks are available. Builders often use face bricks on parts that will show and common brick for parts that will remain hidden. Laying bricks isn't easy for the inexperienced, but adding a brick veneer isn't difficult. It doesn't require as much skill...or patience.

Stucco Stucco, a mixture of cement, sand, lime, and water churned into a thick paste, blends into a natural setting. It's usually applied over lath in three coats, and the finish coat can be applied with a rough texture or nearly smooth. (See "Stuccoing a Wood-Frame Counter," above.) Left uncolored, stucco facing has a soft, subdued appearance. After it dries, it can be painted any color you wish.

Countertops

When selecting a countertop for your outdoor kitchen, go with one that complements the counter base. A cast-concrete countertop on a base with a stone facing provides a handsome rustic look. For something a bit more traditional, try a ceramic-tile countertop with a brick base. If you've clad your base with stucco, a granite countertop will be easy on the eyes. (For information about countertops, see Chapter 7.)

Smart Tip See the Stone

If you are thinking about enclosing your built-in grill with manufactured stone, see the product in person. Visit a showroom to get an accurate reading of color and texture. Take samples home to be sure the product will blend well with your patio and the surrounding site.

Prefabricated Grill Counters

For those who don't want a permanently installed custom-built masonry counter, a prefabricated unit is the next best thing. Prefabricated kitchen counters, confusingly called islands by some manufacturers, are rapidly gaining popularity. They are available in two basic options. The simplest is the ready-made counter, which is available at major home-improvement centers. Or you can select a model from a specialized retailer, choose the finish and countertop, and wait for it to arrive. If you desire a bit more input, a semicustom counter is the way to go. You choose from an assortment of modular units to achieve the counter shape you want. Then, you select from a variety of features, options, countertops, and exterior finishes. Popular countertop choices are porcelain tile and granite. The most common finishes are stone, brick, and stucco, with some companies offering unfinished counters at a reduced cost. Finally, you provide cutout dimensions for the grill and other built-ins. The manufacturer builds the counter, which is typically steel framed, off site according to your specs and delivers it in as little as two weeks. The ease of the process is causing more and more homeowners to consider prefab counters.

Prefab counter options aren't as limited as they were even one year ago. Today, you can get something as modest as a 4-foot square counter with a built-in grill or something as audacious as a 25-foot U-shape unit with a grill, sink, refrigerator, canopy, and auto-rising plasma TV. Even a waterfall is within the realm of possibility. (Note: some prefab counters come with a fully assembled grill and other accessories. Others don't. If they don't, be sure to provide exact cutout dimensions for all the built-in appliances.) As the options for materials and accessories expand, so does the interest in prefab counters.

Making prefab counters even more interesting to prospective buyers are the facts that there is less legwork and less mess. If you go the custom route, prepare to acquire building permits—and prepare to have workers milling about your backyard for weeks, even months. Pre-

fab counters, which are set up stationary on a fixed based or mobile on casters, have some heft, but they can be moved. Store it in the garage over the winter. Take it with you if you move. On average, a prefab counter won't put as big a dent in your wallet, either. Small units can start as low as $2,500, although extravagant designs could cost up to $50,000. Many fall in the $8,000 to $15,000 range. If you can't afford a custom unit or don't have the time and desire to build one yourself, a prefab counter may be your best option.

Don't worry about limitations with pre-fabricated grill counters. This model, opposite, includes a grill, sink, side burner, refrigerator, and raised bar counter.

A prefabricated counter, left, is light enough to rest on most decks and patios without footings. This model, with a tile countertop, provides seating room at the round end of the counter.

Prefabricated Modules

With a variety of modular units available from specialized dealers across the country, you can build an outdoor kitchen counter in the size and shape that you want.

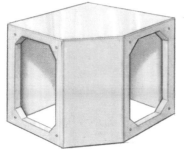

Round   **Crescent**   **Angled**

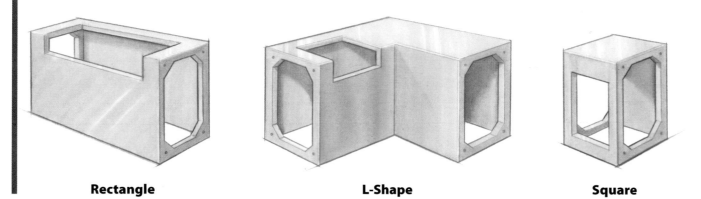

Rectangle   **L-Shape**   **Square**

A small counter, left, may be all you need. This space-saving unit is only 72 in. wide and 33 in. deep, but it still houses a grill and a fridge, and includes storage space. The homeowner opted for a stone facing and a stone-tile countertop.

A custom-built counter will likely require a foundation, but ready-made counters don't. The unit above is light enough to put on a deck.

Allow four weeks lead time for the delivery and setup of prefab counters, such as the U-shape model below.

Bar Islands

When creating your ultimate outdoor kitchen, there is no need to limit yourself to counters. Spice things up a bit by including a bar island in your plans. Aside from being a convenient place from which to dispense beverages, bars are people magnets. A bar island, sometimes referred to as a cocktail station or bartending center, provides the perfect place to chat with guests.

A bar can come in handy by providing a dedicated area for drinks, glasses, shakers, and jiggers, but it doesn't have to be big. Some built-in beverage stations are as small as 14 inches wide. Big or small, an outdoor bar should be functional. Including a stainless-steel sink makes it easier to mix drinks, and it can double as a prep and cleanup area. Storage compartments hold lemons, limes, olives, and other key garnishes, which can be sliced with ease if your bar has a slide-away cutting board. A speed rail, which is a bottle-holding rack, allows you to easily organize and access your wines. Chill those wines in bottle boots and access them with a built-in bottle opener. An insulated ice bin keeps those maraschino cherries cold. If you make a mess, wipe your hands on the towel hanging from the handy towel holder.

If it's too much money to install a bar island, less costly options are available. A bar cart on casters can easily roll right to where the action is. Many manufacturers offer these portable carts with a lot of the features that a built-in bar includes: cutting board, towel rack, compartments for cocktail fixings, and so forth. You can get one with a refrigerator included, but remember that it will have to be plugged into an electrical outlet, so it may not be as easy to move as you'd like. Or go sans fridge. A bar cart can stay cold from the chill of the ice bin.

Much cheaper still is a party cooler on a stand that can keep plenty of drinks cold up to 12 hours. And, of course, there is always the typical cooler. (Look for one with an insulated body that will keep ice for long periods.) Grab it by the handles and you can take it from the outdoor kitchen to the beach, the boat, or your kid's soccer game.

A bar caddy, opposite top, packs plenty of features into a small area. This built-in unit keeps drinks cold in the ice bin, stores garnishes in a handy drawer, and puts bottles within easy reach.

Need some mobility? A portable bar caddy, opposite center, is perfect for beverages, snacks, and condiments. Despite being only 20 in. wide, this model holds up to one hundred 12-oz. cans.

A built-in refreshment center, opposite bottom, has what it takes to keep the party going strong well into the night. It includes a sink, cutting board, condiment bins, high shelf with rails, plenty of storage space, and even a pullout trash container.

The refreshment center, above, is the freestanding version of the built-in one, opposite bottom. Push the stainless-steel unit to a spot by the pool.

Stainless steel, which is easy to keep clean, works great in an outdoor setting. Stainless-steel cabinets are available in standard cabinet sizes. The cabinets in this outdoor kitchen provide tons of storage—and match the drop-in grill.

Cabinets

In recent years, some homeowners have opted for true cabinets, similar to those you'd find indoors, for their outdoor kitchens. These cabinets have a more finished look, offer more usable storage space, and are easier to access than their framed or masonry counterparts.

Indoor kitchen cabinets are typically made of wood, although that is a less popular choice outdoors. Wood has a tendency to expand and contract, and it's subject to mold and mildew. You may install wood cabinets in a warm, dry climate, but you still need to keep them well sealed. It helps if they are under the protection of a roof, awning, or some other overhead structure. And wood is a fire hazard, so keep combustibility in mind at all times.

Stainless-steel cabinets are another popular outdoor-cabinet option. They come complete with drawers and doors and can be installed next to your house, against masonry, or freestanding in an island configuration. Standard base cabinets and sink bases are readily available, though stainless-steel grill bases are more difficult to find and usually have to be made to order. Stainless-steel cabinets are hygienic and easy to keep clean. That's why they are so prevalent in restaurant kitchens, hospitals, and laboratories. They also are impervious to the elements—they won't deteriorate when exposed to ultraviolet rays. If you live by the sea, stainless steel will resist corrosion. Some people love the look of stainless steel. Others think it looks cold. If you're in the latter category, don't worry. Stainless-steel doors and drawers in wood tones are now available.

Cypress cabinet doors work well in this outdoor kitchen, top, because they are sheltered from the two elements that do major damage to wood: the sun and the rain.

Stainless-steel doors, center, don't have to look cold and impersonal. Doors and drawers are available in a variety of wood tones, including mahogany and oak.

The kitchen, which includes a sink base cabinet and a three-door base cabinet, bottom, was constructed of polymer panels. The cabinet doors are made of teak.

Smart Tip

Handle with Care

Cabinets with ornate grooves, detailed moldings, and decorative onlays may add style. They'll also add a degree of difficulty to your cleaning chores, requiring regular care to keep away dirt and grime.

You can have the warm look of wood, without the maintenance.

The latest innovation is outdoor cabinetry. Outdoor cabinet dealers offer units made from marine-grade HDPE (high-density polyethylene), a product engineered for outdoor use that is designed to withstand the elements. It won't warp, crack, rot, peel, or fade when exposed to rain, sleet, or snow. Marine-grade HDPE is a durable polymer that is approved for food contact by the FDA. These out-

door cabinets come in a variety of types, including full-height drawers, three-drawer bases, grill bases, sink bases, end panels, single-door wall units, double-door wall units, and the single-door base, which is the most popular base cabinet. They cost less—about 50 percent less—than stainless steel. Unlike wood, no painting, staining, or sealing is required. When you want to clean the cabinets, simply wash them—inside and out—with a garden hose. They include adjustable legs for sloped or uneven sur-

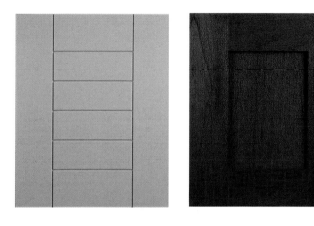

Grill and Burner Base Cabinets

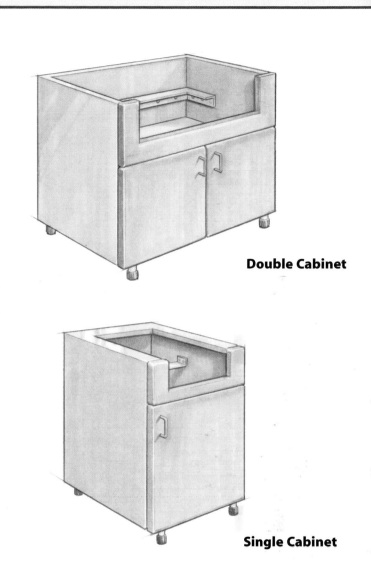

Double Cabinet

Single Cabinet

The sizes of outdoor cabinets vary to fit the built-in grills and side burners of your choice.

This outdoor kitchen, opposite, is perfect for the patio—and a perfect spot to watch the big game at night. The cabinets, which are made of polymer panels, stand up to the harshest elements.

Companies that build outdoor cabinets offer an array of colors and door styles, above, which allow for plenty of design possibilities.

faces. When it gets cold outside, you can store them in the garage. Most come with a lifetime warranty.

Cabinet Sizes

Cabinets come in fairly standard sizes. Base cabinets are 24 inches deep and 34 inches high. When the countertop is added, the cabinet is a standard 36 inches high. Wall cabinets are 12 to 14 inches deep and 12 to 36 inches high. Cabinet widths range from 9 to 60 inches and are typically available in 3-inch increments. The outdoor cabinets come in all the standard sizes, and some companies will build cabinetry to your exact specifications.

Hardware

Hardware, often overlooked when installing cabinetry, is the finishing touch. The door hinges and drawer slides should be sturdy and maintenance free. Door and drawer pulls or knobs should be functional, and they can be personal, too. For functionality, pulls may be easier to use than knobs, especially if you've got your hands full. A tiny knob may be hard to grasp, but a U-shape pull will allow you to open a cabinet with one finger. The only limit when selecting pulls or knobs is your imagination. Lots of people like to match the hardware to the faucet. Many want to introduce an accent color. Others prefer pewter, brass, or copper for an old-fashioned feel. Cabinet hardware in your outdoor kitchen is the perfect opportunity to show off your interests. Try hardware shaped like seashells or butterflies. Perhaps cowboy boots or martini glasses are more your style. Heck, you can even get knobs with the logo of your favorite team. If you've got something in mind, chances are it's out there.

These polymer cabinets, above, come fully assembled and have UV inhibiters for fade resistance.

An outdoor kitchen with teak cabinets, below, can include wall cabinets in addition to the standard base units.

Adjustable legs, below, allow you to level your outdoor cabinets on sloped or uneven surfaces.

Full-extension slides on this cypress drawer, below, are water resistant and can be easily removed for cleaning.

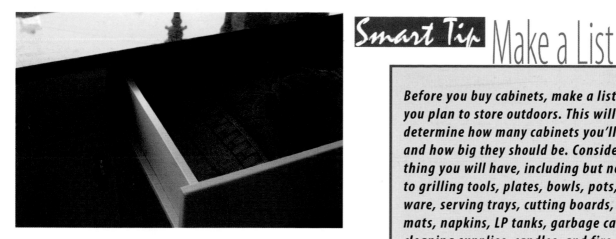

Smart Tip Make a List

Before you buy cabinets, make a list of what you plan to store outdoors. This will help you determine how many cabinets you'll need—and how big they should be. Consider everything you will have, including but not limited to grilling tools, plates, bowls, pots, silverware, serving trays, cutting boards, placemats, napkins, LP tanks, garbage cans, cleaning supplies, candles, and fire extinguishers. Measure everything, too, to be sure planned spaces will accommodate them. No sense installing cabinets that are 12 inches deep to store your favorite 14-inch serving bowls.

The drawers of this outdoor cabinet, above left, were designed without hardware. This way, the slides won't wear out.

To make the most of your space, look for outdoor cabinetry, left, that has full-depth, adjustable shelves with stainless-steel hinges.

A full-extension rollout, below left, makes items more accessible.

If you need to keep certain items out of the hands of children—or nosy guests!—invest in drawers and doors that have locks, below.

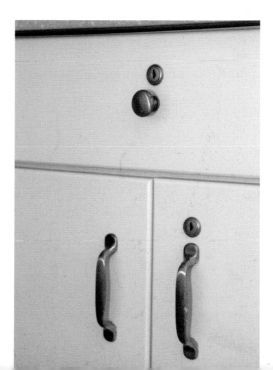

More Storage Ideas

If you've made a list of what you'll need to store (see page 161), you'll know how much storage you'll need, and you'll have a feel for what mix of storage units—cabinets, drawers, and so forth—you'll require. It's always nice to have a little extra storage space, but it's not only about volume. Consider access and organization, too. Having the proper storage will decrease clutter and increase efficiency.

Pullout shelves mounted under the sink or in a base cabinet are practically a must. A pullout shelf that slides on heavy-duty glides keeps supplies handy—and keeps you from having to bend over to reach objects down below. Shelves should roll smoothly, extend fully, and stop automatically so they won't fall out. Use pullout shelves for your LP tank, your trash can, and your large pots. They will help bring these big, bulky objects to the forefront. Your back and knees will thank you.

Another functional item to consider is an under-sink organizer. It fits around the plumbing, making the most of the limited but valuable space you have. An under-sink organizer is the perfect place to keep cleaning supplies.

You've made the most of the space under the sink. Now, think about the unused space in front of the sink. Including a tilt-out tray in your plans will give you the perfect place to hold soap and a sponge. It's also a great spot to put your wedding ring, so you don't have to worry about it falling down the drain while washing vegetables or rinsing dishes.

Simple, easy-to-install organizers on the inside of a door work wonders. Use plastic ones on your base cabi-

A teak console, above, keeps everything you need at hand. It's perfect for serving, storing, and displaying.

This teak buffet, below, would make a great bar station. The drawers and cabinets provide plenty of mobile storage.

Smart Tip Proper Placement

Store items where they'll be used. For example, put mixing bowls and small appliances in the prep area, platters and cutting boards close to the grill, and dish towels and cleaning supplies near the sink.

nets to store canned goods and aluminum foil. Put a spice rack on a unit close to the grill and your pepper and paprika will always be in a convenient locale. For those spots that aren't that convenient to reach, consider a lazy Susan. Get one to fill a corner cabinet—lazy Susans can be circular, half-circular, D-shape, kidney, or pie-cut shape—and you'll utilize a hard-to-reach space.

If you'll be keeping silverware in one of your outdoor drawers, avoid the dreaded drawer debacle by using an organizer tray. These drawer inserts will keep your silverware, cutlery, and miscellaneous utensils organized, allowing you to find what you want, when you want it. If you don't have room in your outdoor space to store all your silverware, consider a cutlery carryall, which is basically an organizer tray with handles, so you can pick it up and carry it outside. For tongs, spatulas, and other oversized grilling utensils that won't fit in a drawer, use a wall-mounted or hanging utensil rack. It's a good spot to hang ladles, cheese graters, whisks, and measuring cups. Some high-end racks have room to store towels, spice canisters, and oil and vinegar bottles. Don't want to install an entire rack? A simple, well-placed peg or hook works great for hanging a potholder, oven mitt, apron, or dish towel.

A chest and a bench are two easy do-it-yourself projects that can provide additional storage space. A storage chest provides easy access to items when opened and serves as a buffet counter or a seat when closed. Build a bench that can store belongings below and you will have a multifunctional piece that saves precious space.

Last, but certainly not least, is the kitchen cart. All storage doesn't have to be built-in. If space is tight, a kitchen cart can store dishes, utensils, towels, and almost anything else you can think of. It's multifunctional, too. It's the perfect place to put an open cookbook as you try out that new recipe. It can double as an extra serving area, and you can even use it as a portable bar. Many of the carts available today are handy and handsome.

Smart Tip Hanging Around

Put unused space to work by hanging pots and pans from a trellis. Do so and you'll reclaim valuable cabinet space. Hang them within easy reach, of course!

A stainless-steel cart, above, provides a perfect place to prep your steaks, burgers, and chicken before you grill.

A full-extension drawer, right, makes it easy to change your LP tank when you run out of fuel.

CHAPTER 9

Set the Stage

OUTDOOR DINING AREAS

No outdoor kitchen is complete without some place to relax and enjoy the food, but the days when a splintery picnic table was the standard are long gone. Today, there are many factors to consider. How much seating will you need? Will one dining space suffice, or will you want to add a snack counter for serving informal meals? How about a bar near the cooking and prep area so the cook has someone to talk with during parties? Is privacy from neighbors an issue?

Furniture selection can have a big impact on the comfort of your guests, too. Oversized stools with armrests and pivoting bases may feel comfortable in the showroom but may be confining once you get them to the patio. Resin or vinyl dining sets may sag under the weight of guests who are large. Big cushions are unlikely to dry quickly after it rains. Sleek, hard-edged, contemporary designs may cause bumps and bruises, especially to children. There are other practical considerations as well. You'll want furniture that's easy to move and store, that can withstand the elements, and that won't require a lot of annual maintenance. Check out your options on the following pages.

As with open floor plans indoors, it's nice to have some separation between cooking and dining areas outdoors, too. Here, long, low planters do the trick.

Where to Dine

Just as indoor dining areas are usually close to the kitchen, you'll want your exterior dining area near your outdoor kitchen. Avoid placement too close to the grill, though, so that smoke and heat do not become annoyances. It may also help to put the dining area upwind of the cooking area so smoky air isn't an issue while dining. Informal eating and drinking areas, such as snack counters and beverage bars, can be put closer to—or be made integral with—the grill counter.

Be attentive to the view diners will have when choosing a site for dining. Avoid locations close to driveways, play structures, or the neighbor's old shed. Also try not to place a dining area so you're not looking at a messy food-prep or cleanup area as you entertain. Privacy considerations may affect your decision as well. Choose a place that's not directly in sight of your neighbors. If that's not possible, consider a privacy screen. (See page 168.) Even a decorative banner or curtain hung on a cable can create some seclusion. Finally, allow plenty of space for traffic. Avoid situations where guests have to pull in their chairs every time someone walks behind them. A separate dining area, such as an alcove or bump-out, is ideal. It can be designed into the shape of the deck or patio or created by positioning a planter or trellis to define the area.

Smart Tip Secondary Seating

If you plan large gatherings, such as a neighborhood barbecue, consider designing your entertainment area with several seating areas rather than one large area. Multiple places to munch promote the circulation of guests. Each should be big enough to seat four (two chairs and a love seat, for example) and include a small table to hold food and drinks. Sometimes wide, flat benches can serve as overflow eating areas, acting as both seats and tables. A snack bar at the back of a food-prep area is convenient for serving quick meals.

Dining areas should be buffered from other activity areas, such as pools. A vine-covered pergola, left, creates a sense of separation even when space is tight.

Eating areas can be arranged in clusters, opposite bottom left, for informal service at large parties.

A snack counter, above, is ideal for serving quick meals. See the photo, right, for a view of the snack counter from inside this outdoor kitchen.

This fully equipped food-prep area, above, is perfect for serving lunches and light snacks, but it can also be used for staging more formal meals.

Privacy Screens and Shades

Outdoor living often means that your neighbors can see you every time you press the ignition button on your grill. If this annoys you, and there's no secluded site for your entertainment area, consider a privacy structure. But don't overdo it or you'll defeat the purpose of having an outdoor entertainment area—enjoying being outside.

Designers have several tricks to create privacy without making you feel claustrophobic. The first is based on a principle that every child knows: you can see out a small hole in a wall, but someone any distance away on the other side can't see inside. Build a structure with lots of "holes," such as a trellis. You and your guests sitting near it will be able to see out without being seen. Another useful trick is to build a privacy wall or overhead structure using boards set at an angle. (See the opposite page.) From your neighbor's house, the wall will look solid, but you will have a view, as well as good air circulation.

Solid balustrades offer privacy when you're seated. Curtains and shades are a lower-cost solution. Canopies, awnings, and hanging umbrellas may help, too. Select a translucent cloth made for outdoor use. While maintaining privacy, it will allow some light to penetrate and make it feel light and airy to those inside.

A rooftop dining area, above, can be partially or completely closed off with outdoor curtains. A nearby lounge area, below, gives guests a place to relax after meals, away from the clutter of dirty dishes.

Slatted wall panels and strings of beads create privacy for this dining area.

Smart Tip Angle for Privacy

A fence built with angled boards, as shown in the drawing, provides privacy when viewed from the nearby house. From the opposite angle (see arrows), however, diners receive light and even have a bit of a view. The angled slats also allow cooling breezes to pass through. For complete privacy, run the angled fence boards horizontally.

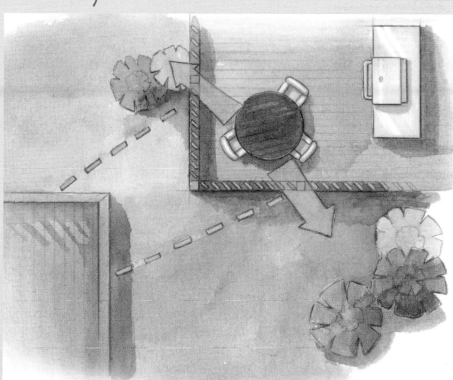

Buying Outdoor Furniture

Before entering an outdoor furniture store, think through your requirements. If your space is limited, for example, be ready to think small in scale. Massive pieces with big armrests and headrests may overpower a small deck or patio. On the other hand, finely wrought furniture may look lost on a large deck built with heavy timbers or a patio built of massive stones.

Whether your area is big or small, versatility is important, too. Choose furnishings that can be arranged for a tête-à-tête or dinner for 12. One successful strategy is to have two tables of the same height; push them together or set them apart as the occasion demands. Whenever possible, choose pieces that are multifunctional, such as a bench that can store cushions below or a table that can expand.

Furniture Materials

Personal taste may rule when it comes to choosing a material, but keep practical considerations in mind here as well. Teak furniture appeals to many homeowners because it does not splinter, is rot resistant, and weathers to a nice silver gray. Many teak sets, however, are too large for small decks or patios—and too costly for many budgets. The latest cast-aluminum designs are attractive, rustproof, and substantial enough for all types of weather while still light enough to move around easily. Like teak, they will cost a little more up front but will last for years. Painted wood and metal are in vogue with homeowners who prefer a casual country feel, but keep in mind that you'll need to repaint regularly. Wrought and cast aluminum are used to create period looks and will last for decades with little maintenance. Tubular aluminum is also formed into furniture styles ranging from Adirondack to contemporary. Another popular trend is "wicker" woven from vinyl-coated wire. It can stay outdoors year-round and cleans easily. Look for models supported by an aluminum rather than steel frame; they're lighter and won't corrode. Natural-wicker furniture may support mold and mildew if allowed to become wet. Furniture made from painted-aluminum tubing is easy to move and often stacks for compact storage. Powder-coated paint finishes tend to be superior to sprayed finishes.

On a Budget?

Check out garage sales in your area. Good-quality outdoor furniture often sells at a fraction of its original cost. You can also find many pieces, including chairs and tables, meant for indoor use that can serve outdoors. Several coats of exterior enamel paint over wood, for example, will last many seasons—especially if you take the furniture in during the winter. Liven up your bargains with new cushions—be sure they're the kind that will dry quickly if left in the rain—and outdoor dining decor, such as tablecloths and placemats. Keep your outdoor furniture clean and make it last by protecting it with vinyl or polyester covers or by stowing it in a shed, especially when it will go unused for a long period.

A large teak table, left, can seat up to 10 diners. Or you can opt for the versatility of two smaller tables, which can be pushed together or pulled apart as needed.

Tables and chairs made of wrought aluminum, right, have a light, delicate look and are well-suited to garden-sited dining areas.

The weathered, rustic look, so popular today, can be bought ready-made, as shown with this teak set, left.

Small, lightweight tables, above, are easy to rearrange as the occasion demands. They're ideal if you prefer to serve meals buffet style.

Furniture Styles

Outdoor furniture comes in many styles. Choose one that either complements your home's style or that fits the theme of your outdoor space. There are rustic pieces that would be at home in front of an Adirondack lodge, ornately wrought-iron and cast-aluminum pieces with English-garden charm, and sets that could be straight off the porch of a Nantucket cottage. Then there are reproductions from the cafés of Europe, designs with Southwestern overtones, bamboo and wicker creations with an Asian sensibility, and minimally styled modern ensembles that nearly disappear and allow the natural setting to have first billing. Beyond dining tables and chairs, there are a host of other furnishings, including bars, end tables, and folding screens, rendered as coordinates, though there's nothing wrong with mixing and matching. As with all furniture, markups are high. It pays to wait for season-ending sales.

Outdoor furniture makers produce more than just tables and chairs. They offer accessory pieces, including tea carts, cabinets, and bars, above.

Wrought-aluminum furniture, below, has the look of furniture from a different century but is space-age light and easy to maintain. It's also very pricey.

This weather-resistant cabinet, right, adds a touch of elegance to any outdoor setting. Use it to store place settings, table linens, and cushions.

Smart Tip Consider the Kids

If you have young children, opt for furniture that doesn't fold, pivot, or tip easily. That way you won't have to worry about kids catching their fingers or chairs overturning. Avoid tables with glass and sharp corners as well.

Wicker made from vinyl-coated wire, above, is almost indistinguishable from the real thing, but it's far more durable and easier to clean.

Building Outdoor Furniture

Building patio furniture is not nearly as demanding as building indoor furniture. You don't need sophisticated tools or skills, finishing is simpler, and the materials are less costly. The table, bench, and chairs shown here are not exceptions. The table can expand to seat six and folds flat for easy transport and storage. So do the chairs.

The table leaves are supported by two triangular braces, left. Lock them in place by inserting the block of wood under each leaf in the notch as shown.

The tabletop, above, is lightweight. Place it on the support and secure it with bolts and wing nuts. Disassembled, the furniture set stores flat against a garage or shed wall.

To fold a chair, above, or bench, lift the seat front and release the screw heads from the key slots. Swing the sides backward and lift the seat front.

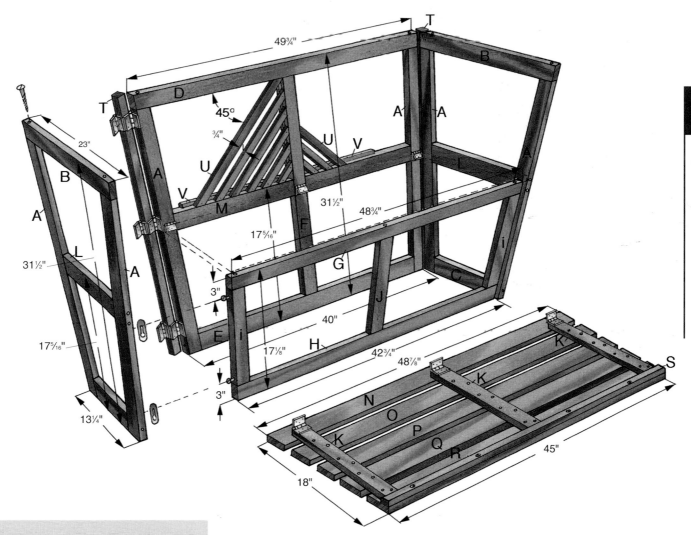

Bench Materials

A: 6 pcs. $\frac{3}{4}$ x $2\frac{1}{2}$ x 31 in.*
B: 2 pcs. $\frac{3}{4}$ x $2\frac{1}{2}$ x 25 in.*
C: 2 pcs. $\frac{3}{4}$ x $2\frac{1}{2}$ x $10\frac{1}{2}$ in.*
D: 1 pc. $\frac{3}{4}$ x $2\frac{1}{2}$ x $51\frac{3}{4}$ in.*
E: 1 pc. $\frac{3}{4}$ x $2\frac{1}{2}$ x 37 in.*
F: 1 pc. $\frac{3}{4}$ x $2\frac{1}{2}$ x $26\frac{1}{2}$ in.
G: 1 pc. $\frac{3}{4}$ x $2\frac{1}{2}$ x $50\frac{3}{4}$ in.*
H: 1 pc. $\frac{3}{4}$ x $2\frac{1}{2}$ x $43\frac{3}{4}$ in.*
I: 2 pcs. $\frac{3}{4}$ x $2\frac{1}{2}$ x 14 in.*
J: 1 pc. $\frac{3}{4}$ x $2\frac{1}{2}$ x $12\frac{1}{8}$ in.
K: 3 pcs. $\frac{3}{4}$ x $1\frac{1}{2}$ x 16 in.
L: 2 pcs. $\frac{3}{4}$ x $2\frac{1}{2}$ x 15 in.*
M: 1 pc. $\frac{3}{4}$ x $2\frac{1}{2}$ x 42 in.*
N: 1 pc. $\frac{3}{4}$ x $3\frac{1}{2}$ x $49\frac{1}{2}$ in.*
O: 1 pc. $\frac{3}{4}$ x $3\frac{1}{2}$ x $48\frac{3}{4}$ in.*
P: 1 pc. $\frac{3}{4}$ x $3\frac{1}{2}$ x 48 in.*
Q: 1 pc. $\frac{3}{4}$ x $3\frac{1}{2}$ x $47\frac{1}{4}$ in.*

R: 1 pc. $\frac{3}{4}$ x $3\frac{1}{2}$ x $46\frac{1}{2}$ in.*
S: 1 pc. $\frac{3}{4}$ x $\frac{3}{4}$ x $45\frac{3}{4}$ in.*
T: 2 pcs. $\frac{3}{4}$ x $\frac{3}{4}$ x $33\frac{1}{2}$ in.*
U: $\frac{1}{4}$ x $\frac{3}{4}$ in. x 56 ft.**
V: $\frac{1}{4}$ x $\frac{1}{2}$ in. x 24 ft.**

Miscellaneous: $\frac{3}{8}$-in. dowel (1); $1\frac{1}{2}$ x 2-in. (opened) hinges (18); $\frac{9}{16}$ x $1\frac{11}{16}$-in. keyhole fittings (4); No. 6 round head screws (6 @ $1\frac{1}{4}$ in.); No. 6 screws ($1\frac{1}{4}$, 2 in.); No. 16 brads ($\frac{3}{4}$ in.); exterior wood glue; wood putty; primer; paint

* Oversize (about 2 in.) pieces require additional cutting

** Total length, cut to fit

Key slots lock chairs and the bench in the open position while in use. Bore small recesses behind the key slots prior to screwing them into place.

CHAPTER 10

Make Yourself Comfortable

FINISHING TOUCHES

Once you have taken care of the basics, such as appliances, cabinetry, fixtures, and furniture, there are lots of extras you can add to your outdoor living space to make it feel as comfortable as the rest of your home. Wireless speakers, for example, allow you to flip burgers to the beat of your favorite tunes. All-weather LCD televisions, available in a variety of sizes, let you tune in to your favorite show after the meal. Even DVD/VCR players have been weatherized. Outdoor phones, radios, and clocks are a few other familiar conveniences that you can add to your open-air living space.

The outdoor living phenomenon has also given rise to products for outdoor decorating. Carpeting, curtains, shades, blinds, cushions, and furniture, for example, have been redesigned to withstand the elements. And don't forget outdoor lighting. There is an endless selection, including mood-enhancing gas lanterns that operate with the flick of a wall switch and LED lights that glow for so many hours you'll be willing them to your kids. You will find the full range of options on the following pages, as well as where to buy them in the Resource Guide, which begins on page 212.

Outdoor curtains offer some protection from wind, rain, and sun while creating privacy with a soft, graceful look.

Outdoor curtains are a graceful and animated addition to an outdoor room. In very breezy weather, they may need to be weighted or tied.

bunch, or get underfoot the way curtains can. In addition, shades and blinds almost disappear when you don't need them for privacy or sun protection.

When choosing your shades, keep in mind color, thickness of fabric, and tightness of the weave. Light colors provide the best heat rejection, while dark colors absorb light for better glare control. Some companies sell combination shades, with the light side facing out and the dark side facing in. A loose weave allows for air circulation and for some light to pass through the shade. Heavy fabrics resist wind better.

The best fabric options for outdoor shades are non-stretch polyester coated with PVC, fiberglass coated with PVC polymers, UV-stabilized polyethylene, or solution-dyed acrylic. PVC-coated, nonstretch polyester resists flame, fade, and mildew, and is durable. It repels the sun's rays and heat, washes clean easily with soap and water, and comes with a 10- to 15-year warranty. Fiberglass treated with PVC polymers is another durable option. It is resistant to the weather and fading. The porous quality of the fabric gives superb transparency for both ventilation and muted views. A drawback to fiberglass fabric is it can tear easier than many other fabrics. Shades made of knitted, UV-stabilized polyethylene fibers also stand up to the weather. They can block up to 90 percent of UV rays yet allow air through because of the loose weave. This allows light to filter in and for you to see out. Polyethylene fabrics are colorfast. They won't support mold or mildew, rot, shrink, fade, fray, or tear—even in extreme weather conditions. If color and design are important, then solution-dyed acrylic fabric, available in more than 60 colors and 80 patterns, gives you the most options. Solution-dyed fabrics are dyed as the fiber is being made, before being woven, so the color goes completely through the fiber. A protective finish offers resistance to oils, dirt, stains, water, and mildew, and blocks the sun's rays. This fabric comes with a five-year warranty.

All brackets and attachments for these shades should be made of stainless steel to prevent rusting and are mounted on either stainless-steel or aluminum rollers. Add side channels to keep shades stationary in windy conditions, or choose from a variety of tie downs.

Blinds offer more sun control than either curtains or shades and, like the other options, are available in abundant variety. With a relatively small investment, you can have tajonal or bamboo blinds. Tajonal is a native plant of the Yucatan that grows straight and is chocolate in color. It looks a lot like a brown bamboo, and its stalks are finger size. Bamboo shades come in many hues of caramel as well as a variety of earth tones. Both varieties are constructed with tough nylon cord and varnished with UV-resistant polyurethane to better withstand the elements. You can also purchase blinds with red cedar slats or metal fins. Either adds a nice, contemporary look and allows you to adjust the slat angle to control the amount of light, privacy, and airflow you desire. Want something even more substantial? Consider shutters with adjustable slats. They are available in various woods and plastics and come in many sizes.

Cushions and carpets, opposite, are made to withstand sun and rain, and to dry quickly after a shower, too.

Cushions

Cushions add a warm welcome and comfort to any outdoor room. Buy them ready-made in many shapes or sizes as needed for existing furniture, or have them custommade to suit your furnishings and your decorating theme. Fabrics range from cotton canvas and polyester to acrylic fibers. All of these fast-drying fabrics are treated to repel water and resist fades, but they will last a lot longer if covered or brought inside during inclement weather. Filled with mildew-resistant polyurethane foam, these cushions can weather an occasional dousing when forgotten during a rainstorm.

Outdoor shades, in addition to being adjustable, can block varying amounts of light, depending on the openness of the material.

Craftsman-Style Garden Kitchen

Cook and dine in any weather in this beautifully crafted outdoor kitchen and matching screen house. The cooking area, which abuts a small barn, is protected by a roof that's deep enough to keep the cook dry, too. Cedar cabinetry, a concrete countertop, and a built-in microwave, refrigerator, and large grill facilitate preparation of everything from a snack to a full meal. The track-hung folding doors disappear completely when open. Opposite the kitchen are a rock garden, an ornamental pool, and a screen house that's set up for bug-free dining. The decorative woodwork on the cabinets and kitchen doors echo the details of the screen house.

The compact design of this kitchen, right, includes a polished and permanently sealed concrete countertop, below, cedar cabinets, a grill, and a fridge.

Enclosure doors, left, fold to the inside and disappear against the side walls when in the fully open position.

When closed, the pattern on the doors, below left, matches the one used over the screen panels on the screen house, opposite top and bottom.

Folding doors hang on horizontal rollers, below, and a header-mounted track that's unaffected by dirt and debris on the ground.

A rock garden with low-voltage path lighting, a man-made stream, and a pool, above, fill the area between the outdoor kitchen and the screen house.

The screen house, right, which has 120-volt electrical service, is built of cedar on a platform deck. It's a short stroll from the outdoor kitchen.

Passing Through

A covered porch is one of the most sensible of all locations for an outdoor kitchen. It protects countertops, cabinets, and appliances from the weather. In the case of this kitchen, that includes a grill, sink, refrigerator, beverage cooler, warming drawers, and a dishwasher! A porch kitchen is easily accessible from both the house and the yard. Here, a pass-through allows the owners to move ingredients for meals quickly to the outdoor cooking area. Windows that slide and fold, similar to the way a bifold door works, were used to create the pass-through opening. Prepared dishes are in turn easily moved from the porch kitchen to the snack bar.

Other things to like about this kitchen? The grill is well out of the traffic paths, and a range hood prevents smoke from becoming a problem. An awning can cover the snack area if it's too sunny or in case of a drizzle. Larger parties can be staged on the other end of the porch or grade-level patio. To top it all off, the porch roof doubles as a support for a bedroom balcony.

A pass-through from the kitchen, below, reduces the number of trips through the back door. An awning protects diners from sun and showers.

The extended eave, right, adds shelter for this porch-based kitchen. It also provides support for the second-story balcony above.

Despite its compact size, this outdoor kitchen, left, offers plenty of counter and storage space.

A stone wall, above, encloses the snack area and minimizes the impact of the outdoor kitchen on the house's elevation.

A handrail and guardrail, left, detailed to match the house, keep guests safe when ascending steps and using the deck.

Hiring a Contractor

If you're planning to hire a contractor to build your outdoor kitchen, be sure to hire one that's reputable. The best candidates have been in business for at least a few years and have experience installing outdoor kitchens. They will need to be knowledgeable about all of the relevant trades, including electrical, plumbing, carpentry, and, often, masonry. Request references, and check that his workman's compensation and liability insurance are up to date. If the contractor won't be doing the actual work, find out who will be (an employee or subcontractor, for example).

Ask for a contract that, in addition to total cost, specifies products to be used, start and completion dates, cleanup standards at the end of each workday, and how change orders will be handled. (Change orders occur when you change your mind about some aspect of the job midstream.) In addition, discuss how the job will be handled. For example, who will reseed or sod the lawn around a newly installed deck or patio? Who is responsible for disposing of old building materials and waste? Will the contractor supply portable facilities for his crew, or will he want access to your bathroom? It's best to meet with several contractors before signing a contract with the one who, all things considered, you think will do the best job for a reasonable amount of money.

Going Below Deck

Another well-protected place for outdoor kitchens and dining areas is under a second-story deck. Such spaces, often underused, provide shelter from sun and wind, and can be easily screened to keep out insects. But you'll need to install an under-deck drainage system, available from several manufacturers, to keep it dry. (See the illustration.)

Most under-deck drainage systems consist of rounded or V-shaped channels that are inserted between deck joists. They collect the rainwater that seeps between the deck boards and direct it to a center or side gutter. From there, it runs to one or more leaders (downspouts). The better systems are made of vinyl or aluminum and allow air to circulate beneath the deck boards, lessening the chance of rot and mildew. Be sure the components are sturdy enough to hold up should collected water freeze during the colder months. If you don't like the look of the system, you can cover much of it with something more decorative, such as cedar or bead-board. Allow for access to the gutter, however, as you may have to clean it out from time to time. With a dry area below, you open up many possibilities, including the installation of a ceiling fan, lighting, other outdoor kitchen amenities, and the use of comfortable indoor types of furnishings that would otherwise be ruined by the weather.

Under-Deck Drainage System

Rain that passes through the decking is channeled to a gutter and then to a downspout.

This outdoor cooking and dining area, above, is below a second-story deck. It stays dry during all but the most driving rainstorms.

By channeling away rainwater, you can use the ceiling for lighting and fans, left, without having to worry about the fixtures getting soaked.

Rolling Along

This compact, low-cost outdoor kitchen features a built-in grill, a sink, plenty of work surface, a tabletop with room for four to six diners, a storage cabinet, and a shelf. Center holes provide support for a large shade umbrella. The unit folds to a compact size and has wheels so you can roll it to various places in your yard. Move it under a favorite tree when it's in bloom or into the sun when it's chilly. When the season is over, roll it into a garage or storage shed.

Many small charcoal, gas, or electric grills can be adapted for use in this project. The grill you choose should measure about 10 x 18 inches. If you opt for a charcoal grill, bolt corner braces to it so it hangs in the opening and can be lifted out for cleaning. Screws act as pins to hold it in position and maintain a 1-inch gap between the grill and the tabletop to prevent scorching. Alternately, grills with legs can sit directly on the recessed top of the storage cabinet, provided that guide blocks are screwed to the cabinet top to ensure proper position of the grill. You can, of course, opt not to cut out an opening for the grill and to simply use the supplied legs to stand it on the table.

When the unit is not being used for dining, it's still handy for meal preparation. Garden vegetables can be

If you're tired of hosting backyard parties where you spend most of the time running back and forth to the kitchen or tending a lonely grill, put the kitchen where the company is and join the fun!

trimmed and washed in the sink before bringing them into the house. And there is a lot of space around the grill to make barbecuing a pleasure.

The sink can be either an under-mount or drop-in style. Install with sealant and clips as recommended by the manufacturer. Depending on the sink you choose, the faucet will be mounted either behind the sink or through a drilled hole in the top, as shown.

Water for the sink comes from a garden hose that can be snapped on and off with quick-connect hose couplings. On a sunny day, coil the supply hose in a sunny place and you'll have solar-heated water for rinsing dishes. The sink's drain hose can be directed to a garden bed or, if you're using detergent, to a bucket that can be emptied later. (For a materials list and directions for building this outdoor kitchen, see page 209.)

When the rolling kitchen is not in use, store it in a dry place or under a tarp. With flaps folded, right, the outdoor kitchen measures only 26 x 48 in.

KITCHENS FOR EVERY BUDGET

The cabinet under the grill, above, is big enough to hold dishes, utensils, and everything else you need to cook and serve a simple meal.

With everything happening outdoors, you'll find that your guests are happy to lend a hand. Even peeling vegetables can be fun when it happens in the open, above.

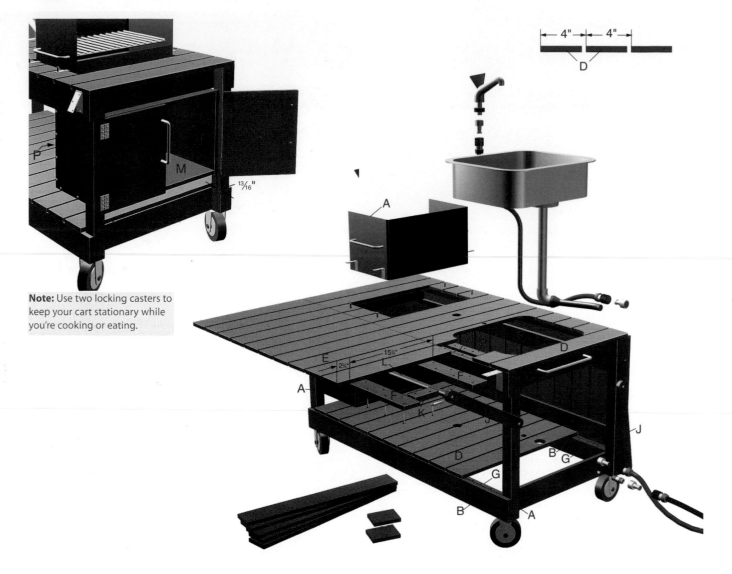

Note: Use two locking casters to keep your cart stationary while you're cooking or eating.

Rolling Kitchen Materials

A: 4 pcs. 1½ x 1½ x 23 in.

B: 4 pcs. ¾ x 3½ x 51½ in.

C: 4 pcs. ¾ x 3½ x 24 in.

D: 24 pcs. ¾ x 3½ x 25½ in.

E: 26 pcs. ¾ x 3½ x 20½ in.

F: 4 pcs. ¾ x 3½ x 51½ in.

G: 2 pcs. ¾ x ¾ x 47 in.

H: 2 pcs. ¾ x 1½ x 47 in.

J: 4 pcs. ¾ x 1½ x 16 in.

K: 4 pcs. ¾ x 1½ x 4 in.

L: 1 pc. ¾-in.-dia. x 51⅞ in.

M: 2 pcs. ¾ x 13 x 19½ in.

N: 2 pcs. ¾ x 13 x 15¼ in.

P: 1 pc. ¾ x 15¼ x 19½ in.

Q: 2 pcs. ¾ x 10⅜ x 16¾ in.

Miscellaneous: grill (approximately 10 x 18 in.); bar sink; faucet; misc. water and drain fittings and connectors; cabinet pulls (2); 12-in. towel bar; 2-in. angle brackets to hang grill (4); No. 6 screws (1⅛, 1½ in.); hinges for doors (4) and drop leaves (4); casters with 4-in.-dia. wheels (2); locking casters with 4-in.-dia. wheels (2)

Building a Compact Rolling Kitchen

1 Precut all parts according to the drawing and the dimensions specified in the materials list, and assemble the frame using 2-in. screws and waterproof glue.

2 Install the tabletop and shelf boards D and leaf boards E and F. Use ³/₁₆-in. spacers between boards for consistent spacing. Leave an opening for the grill, or use a tabletop grill instead.

3 Mark the sink opening as directed by the sink manufacturer, and cut it out using a saber saw. Drill or cut holes for the faucet, outlet, hoses, umbrella pole, and supply and drain hoses.

4 With the table on its top, attach leaves to rails B using six hinges. Screw stop blocks K under the leaves as shown. Turn-buttons secure the brace to the tabletop when it is in the open position.

5 Assemble the cabinet using waterproof glue and screws. Paint and mount it 1½ in. above the shelf, ¾ in. back from the face of the legs. Mount the doors using galvanized hinges and screws.

6 Quick-connect hose couplers make it easy to connect or disconnect the sink's water supply and drain hoses.

A semicircular deck around the snack bar, above, provides a firm footing for stools. Or you may build this kitchen on a deck or patio. Free plans are available from The Engineered Wood Association (APA). (See the Resource Guide.)

Prepare meals with the shades up or down, right. A plastic laminate counter runs the length of the enclosure.

Outdoor Kitchen Pavilion

This multipurpose building accommodates an electric grill and cooking necessities in summer and stores outdoor furniture in winter. The design is best located along one edge of a patio or deck. The architect chose plywood siding to keep construction easy and costs low. Paint it to match the color scheme of your house or surrounding elements, such as fencing. Cover the openings with fiberglass screening, and use outdoor fabric for the door and window shades. The counter's base has a quarry tile curb so it can withstand the abuse of scuffing shoes and inclement weather.

The kitchen's interior was designed to make cleanup easy. Quarry tiles were used for the floor, and plastic laminate covers all counter, shelf, and cabinet surfaces. Interior walls are rough-sawn plywood. The cupola has a plastic glazing panel roof to help ensure a well-lit working area.

If you want to use a propane grill in this structure, the design of the building should be modified. The National Fire Protection Association codes state that propane grills should only be used outdoors; to be considered "outdoors," an enclosure must be at least 50 percent open. To achieve this, the area of the side windows must be doubled. Vents at floor level would be advisable as well. (Propane is heavier than air and could dissipate through the vents should there be a leak.) Under no circumstance should a pavilion containing a gas grill be closed in with glass or plastic installed over window, vent, and door openings. Check with your local building department for other restrictions that may apply.

The bar counter, above, is just big enough to seat four for dinner. Stone or wood makes a suitable surface material.

Base cabinets and shelves, above, allow you to store everything you need for cooking and for service.

11

KITCHENS FOR EVERY BUDGET

Kitchen in a Shed

In less than 30 square feet, you can have a permanent outdoor cooking station complete with a roof, grill, sink, and cabinets. Lattice panels allow you to use the back of the kitchen for hanging implements. Simply choose a corner of your deck or patio that's out of traffic paths and downwind from your dining area. No footings are necessary. Nor do you need sophisticated woodworking skills or tools.

One of the best features of this project is the outdoor sink. With a little ingenuity, there's no need to bring dishes inside for cleanup after the meal. The water supply is made using snap-together hose couplings and is fastened to the tap with a clamp. When the outdoor kitchen is in use, simply take the garden hose and connect it to the coupling.

The outlet is a matching hose connected to the drain.

The transition from the drainpipe to the garden hose is made with a piece of bicycle tube. One end is stretched over the drainpipe and clamped. The other end gets clamped to a length of hose. A piece of copper pipe is tapped inside the garden hose to make it strong enough to withstand clamping. You may drain water into a drywell or gravel-filled pit. Just be sure to use only a biodegradable detergent. Or drain wastewater to a container.

Many types of grills can be used for this outdoor kitchen. Allow a gap of at least 1 inch from the grill to the countertop to prevent scorching the wood, or use a fire-resistant backer board. The grill hangs from four small brackets, which are bolted to the grill sides. Pins, fashioned from screws with the heads cut off, allow for precise placement of the grill as well as easy removal for cleaning. (For a materials list and directions for building the kitchen in a shed, see page 210.)

The wash table, left, is made of larch-wood boards treated with linseed oil.

The cabinets, below, are watertight and easily removed during the off-season. Keep them in position with small screws. Pitch the cabinet tops slightly to promote runoff. The bottom-hinged doors allow easy access because they are never in the way.

A compact kitchen shed, opposite, keeps preparation to a minimum. Everything is at your fingertips.

Make the drain for the sink from a bicycle tire tube, above. Knock a piece of metal pipe into the hose so the tube can be tightened around the hose with a clamp.

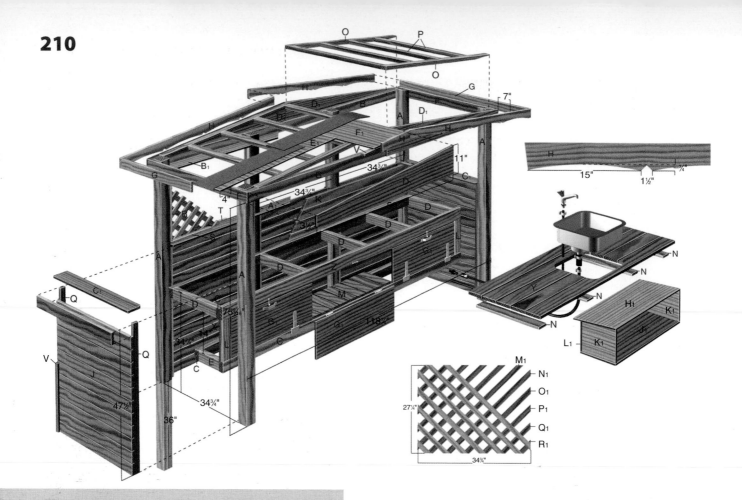

Kitchen in a Shed Materials

A: 4 pcs. $3\frac{1}{2}$ x $3\frac{1}{2}$ in. x 10 ft. *

B: 2 pcs. $1\frac{1}{2}$ x $3\frac{1}{2}$ in. x 9 ft. $10\frac{1}{4}$ in.

C: 3 pcs. $1\frac{1}{2}$ x $3\frac{1}{2}$ in. x 9 ft. $7\frac{1}{4}$ in.

D: 5 pcs. $1\frac{1}{2}$ x $3\frac{1}{2}$ x 20 in.

E: 5 pcs. $1\frac{1}{2}$ x $3\frac{1}{2}$ x 11 in.

F: 2 pcs. $\frac{3}{4}$ x $3\frac{1}{2}$ x 45 in.

G: 2 pcs. $\frac{3}{4}$ x $3\frac{1}{2}$ x 59 in.

H: 4 pcs. $\frac{3}{4}$ x $3\frac{1}{2}$ x $66\frac{3}{4}$ in.

J: 60 pcs. $\frac{3}{4}$ x $3\frac{1}{2}$ x $34\frac{3}{4}$ in.

K: 4 pcs. $\frac{3}{4}$ x $3\frac{1}{2}$ x 9 ft. $3\frac{1}{4}$ in.

L: 2 pcs. $1\frac{1}{8}$ x $3\frac{1}{2}$ x 14 in.

M: 9 pcs. $\frac{3}{4}$ x $3\frac{1}{2}$ x $13\frac{1}{4}$ in.

N: 8 pcs. $\frac{3}{4}$ x $3\frac{1}{2}$ x $19\frac{1}{2}$ in.

O: 4 pcs. $1\frac{1}{2}$ x $2\frac{1}{2}$ x $55\frac{1}{2}$ in.

P: 8 pcs. $1\frac{1}{2}$ x $2\frac{1}{2}$ x $39\frac{3}{4}$ in.

Q: 10 pcs. $1\frac{1}{8}$ x 2 x $47\frac{1}{2}$ in.**

R: 6 pcs. $1\frac{1}{8}$ x $1\frac{1}{8}$ x $27\frac{1}{4}$ in.

S: 6 pcs. $1\frac{1}{8}$ x $1\frac{1}{8}$ x $32\frac{1}{2}$ in.

T: 6 pcs. $\frac{1}{2}$ x $1\frac{1}{8}$ x $32\frac{1}{2}$ in.

U: 6 pcs. $\frac{1}{2}$ x $1\frac{1}{8}$ x $27\frac{1}{4}$ in. ***

V: 10 pcs. $\frac{1}{2}$ x $1\frac{1}{8}$ x $47\frac{1}{2}$ in.

W: 4 pcs. $\frac{3}{4}$ x $1\frac{1}{2}$ x $64\frac{3}{8}$ in.

X: 2 pcs. $\frac{3}{4}$ x $1\frac{1}{2}$ x 14 in.

Y: 4 pcs. $1\frac{1}{8}$ x $5\frac{1}{2}$ in. x 9 ft. $7\frac{1}{4}$ in.

Z: 1 pc. $1\frac{1}{8}$ x $4\frac{5}{8}$ x 9 ft. $7\frac{1}{4}$ in.****

A1: 1 pc. $1\frac{1}{8}$ x $5\frac{1}{2}$ x 9 ft. $3\frac{1}{4}$ in.

B1: 1 pc. $1\frac{1}{8}$ x $5\frac{1}{2}$ x 9 ft. $10\frac{1}{4}$ in.

C1: 2 pcs. $1\frac{1}{8}$ x $3\frac{1}{2}$ x $34\frac{3}{4}$ in.

D1: 4 pcs. $\frac{3}{4}$ x 11 x $59\frac{7}{8}$ in.

E1: 2 pcs. $\frac{3}{4}$ x 48 x 59 in.

F1: 2 pcs. $\frac{3}{4}$ x $16\frac{3}{8}$ x 59 in.

G1: 3 pcs. $\frac{3}{4}$ x $13\frac{7}{8}$ x $39\frac{13}{16}$ in.

H1: 1 pc. $\frac{3}{4}$ x 15 x $35\frac{7}{8}$ in.

J1: 1 pc. $\frac{3}{4}$ x $13\frac{1}{2}$ x $35\frac{7}{8}$ in.

K1: 2 pcs. $\frac{3}{4}$ x to suit x $12\frac{3}{4}$ in.*****

L1: 1 pc. $\frac{3}{4}$ x to suit x $35\frac{7}{8}$ in.*****

M1: 6 pcs. $\frac{3}{4}$ x $1\frac{1}{2}$ x $40\frac{3}{4}$ in.

N1: 12 pcs. $\frac{3}{4}$ x $1\frac{1}{2}$ x $37\frac{3}{8}$ in.

O1: 12 pcs. $\frac{3}{4}$ x $1\frac{1}{2}$ x $29\frac{1}{2}$ in.

P1: 12 pcs. $\frac{3}{4}$ x $1\frac{1}{2}$ x $21\frac{5}{8}$ in.

Q1: 12 pcs. $\frac{3}{4}$ x $1\frac{1}{2}$ x $13\frac{3}{4}$ in.

R1: 12 pcs. $\frac{3}{4}$ x $1\frac{1}{2}$ x $5\frac{15}{16}$ in.

S1: 4 pcs. $\frac{5}{4}$ x $\frac{5}{4}$ x $64\frac{3}{8}$ in.******

Miscellaneous: T-hinges (6); door handles (3); No. 6 screws ($1\frac{1}{2}$, 2, $2\frac{1}{2}$, $2\frac{3}{4}$ in.); No. 8 screws (3 in.); 4d galva-

nized finishing nails; rolled roofing (1 roll); 10.3-oz. tubes roofing cement (6); $\frac{3}{4}$-in. roofing nails; 15 x 15 x 7-in. sink; sink clips (4); faucet; misc. water and drain fittings and connectors; primer; paint; varnish

* Oversize (about 1 ft.) pieces require additional cutting after installation

** Rip from $\frac{5}{4}$ x 4 in.

*** Exterior vertical lattice stops (not shown)

**** Rip from $\frac{5}{4}$ x 6 in.

***** Measure height for storage box after installing sink. Size additional storage boxes to suit need and space beneath the counter.

****** Triangular pieces (not shown) to cover roofing seams at H. Install in a bed of caulk.

Building a Kitchen in a Shed

1 Dig 3-ft.-deep holes for the uprights A using a posthole digger. Place the uprights in holes; plumb; and support them temporarily with bottom rails and cross braces. Fill the holes and tamp.

2 Assemble five siding panels by screwing the boards J onto the cleats Q. Screw the panels between the uprights 1 or 2 in. off the ground with the cleats flush to the inside of the uprights.

3 Screw boards B and F to the posts A after removing the braces. Make cuts for the posts into boards A1 and B1. Screw A1 atop the back siding panel. B1 installs under B. Install boards D.

4 Assemble the roof framing. Cut off the tops of the middle posts A level with the top edge of B. Cut out the gable boards D1, and screw to B. Cut the corner post flush to the gable tops.

5 Screw the roof framing assemblies between the gables, and then screw on the roof sheathing. Cover the roof with roofing felt.

6 Assemble the tabletop base, and install it at a height of 36 in. Assemble and install the countertop boards. Trace and cut the hole for the sink. Then install the lower shelf, and build the cabinets.

RESOURCE GUIDE

The following list of manufacturers and associations is meant to be a general guide to additional industry and product-related sources. It is not intended as a listing of products and manufacturers represented by the photographs in this book.

Advanced Concrete Enhancement
11070 Fleetwood St., Unit F
Sun Valley, CA 91352
818-504-0424
www.aceconrete.com
Manufactures decorative concrete kitchen sinks, counter-tops, surrounds, and flooring.

Andersen Corporation
100 Fourth Ave. North
Bayport, MN 55003-1096
800-426-4261
www.andersenwindows.com
Offers a full line of patio doors and windows.

APA – The Engineered Wood Association
7011 South 19th St.
Tacoma, WA 98466
253-565-6600
www.apawood.org
A nonprofit trade association that represents manufacturers of a variety of engineered-wood products. Offers a full plan for the outdoor kitchen on pages 206-207. Download it free of charge from the association's Web site.

AridDek
1604 Athens Hwy.
Gainesville, GA 30507
877-270-9387
www.ariddek.com
Manufactures aluminum decking and railings.

Arthur Lauer, Inc.
47 Steve's Ln.
Gardiner, NY 12525
845-255-2015
www.arthurlauer.com
Offers several lines of outdoor teak furniture, as well as rugs, pillows, and other products for outdoor living.

Atlantis Cabinetry
3304 Aerial Way Dr.
Roanoke, VA 24018
540-342-0363

www.atlantiscabinetry.com
Manufactures durable, polymer outdoor cabinetry in a variety of colors and designs.

Baldwin Lawn Furniture
440 Middlefield St.
Middletown, CT 06457
800-344-5103
www.baldwinfurniture.com
Builds outdoor furniture, planters, and pergolas.

Barbeques Galore
10 Orchard Rd., Ste. 200
Lake Forest, CA 92630
800-752-3085
www.bbqgalore.com
Retailer of barbecue grills, cooking islands, and accessories.

Blue Rhino Corporation
104 Cambridge Plaza Dr.
Winston-Salem, NC 27104
800-762-1142
www.uniflame.com
Offers a full line of grills, heaters, and other outdoor appliances, plus a propane tank exchange program.

CableRail/Feeney Architectural Products
2603 Union St.
Oakland, CA 94607
800-888-2418
www.cablerail.com
Manufactures a line of standard and custom cable assemblies for deck railings and trellis systems.

Cal Spas
1462 East Ninth St.
Pomona, CA 91766
800-225-7727
www.calspas.com
Manufactures barbecue grills, islands, modular islands, fire pits, and fireplaces for the outdoors.

Char-Broil
1442 Belfast Ave.

Columbus, GA 31904
706-571-7000
www.charbroil.com
Manufactures all types of grills, fireplaces, and accessories.

Chicago Specialty Gardens

1234 Sherman Ave.
Evanston, IL 60202
847-425-1715
www.chicagogardens.com
Full-service firm that specializes in creating rooftop kitchens and entertainment areas.

Classic Garden Design

1 Katydid Ln.
Weston, CT
203-226-2886
www.classicgardendesign.com
Designs and installs residential patios, perennial gardens, pergolas, walks, fences, and outdoor kitchens.

Classic Home Elements

540 Gleason Dr.
Moosic, PA 18507
570-774-0057
www.classichomeelements.com
Manufactures outdoor teak and polymer cabinets.

Concrete Encounter

419 Knapps Hwy.
Fairfield, CT 06825
203-659-4765
www.concreteencounter.com
Manufactures concrete countertops, custom sinks, fireplace surrounds, and precast elements.

ConcreteNetwork.com

31776 Yucaipa Blvd., Ste. 3
Yucaipa, CA 92399
866-380-7754
www.conretenetwork.com
Comprehensive online resource—for homeowners and contractors—for information on working with concrete.

Conrad Imports, Inc.

600 Townsend St., Ste. 400W
San Francisco, CA 94103-5687
415-626-3303
www.conradshades.com
Creates handwoven window coverings made from natural fibers for indoor and outdoor use.

Consumer Product Safety Commission (CPSC)

4330 East West Hwy.
Bethesda, MD 20814
800-638-2772
www.cpsc.gov
Organization charged with protecting the public from unreasonable risks of serious injury or death from more than 15,000 types of consumer products.

Coolaroo

P.O. Box 951509
Lake Mary, FL 32795-1509
800-560-4667
www.coolaroo.com
Manufactures shade sails, umbrellas, and other shade devices that feature knitted outdoor fabric.

Country Casual

7601 Rickenbacker Dr.
Gaithersburg, MD 20879
800-289-8325
www.countrycasual.com
Designs and manufactures teak garden furniture, including dining tables, benches, and chairs.

Cunningham Living

18700 Carrot St.
Spring, TX 77391
800-833-5998
www.cunninghamliving.com
Builds custom outdoor kitchens and offers outdoor appliances, cabinets, and accessories.

Dacor

1440 Bridge Gate Dr.
Diamond Bar, CA 91765
800-793-0093
www.dacor.com
Designs and manufactures a full line of outdoor grills, built-in grills, grill carts, warming ovens, and side burners.

Danver

One Grand St.
Wallingford, CT 06492
888-441-0537
www.danver.com
Produces stainless-steel kitchen cabinets and carts for the outdoors.

DCS by Fisher & Paykel

5900 Skylab Rd.

Huntington Beach, CA 92647
888-936-7872
www.dcsappliances.com
Offers a full line of stainless-steel outdoor grills and grilling systems, including sinks, side burners, and griddles.

Dry-B-Lo
475 Tribble Gap Rd., Ste. 305
Cumming, GA 30040
800-437-9256
www.dry-b-lo.com
Manufactures aluminum deck-drainage systems that keep the space below decks dry.

Earthstone Wood-Fire Ovens
6717 San Fernando Rd.
Glendale, CA 91201
800-840-4915
www.earthstoneovens.com
Offers a full line of preassembled and modular wood- and gas-fired ovens.

Eldorado Stone
31610 NE 40th St.
Carnation, WA 98014
425-883-1991
www.eldoradostone.com
Manufactures veneer stone for outdoor use.

EverGrain Composite Decking, a div. of TAMKO Building Products, Inc.
P.O. Box 1404
Joplin, MO 64802
800-253-1401
www.evergrain.com
Manufactures composite decking products with realistic, compression-molded graining patterns.

Fire Magic
14724 East Proctor Ave.
City of Industry, CA 91746
800-332-0240
www.rhpeterson.com
Manufactures infrared grills and other outdoor kitchen components.

Fire Stone Home Products
12400 Portland Ave. South, Ste. 195
Burnsville, MN 55337
866-303-4028
www.firestonehp.com

Offers a full product line for outdoor living, including grills, fireplaces, lighting, and furniture.

First Impressions Mid-Atlantic, Inc.
P.O. Box 2102
Chesapeake, VA 23327
888-548-9981
www.firstimpressionsnet.com
Offers gas and electric outdoor lighting.

Fogazzo Wood Fired Ovens and Barbecues
114 East St. Joseph Ave.
Arcadia, CA 91006
866-364-2996
www.fogazzo.com
Designs and manufactures wood-fired ovens, barbecues, and fireplaces for the outdoors.

Forno Bravo
399 Business Park Crt., #104
Windsor, CA 95492
800-407-5119
www.fornobravo.com
Manufactures gas- and wood-fired pizza ovens.

Frigidaire
250 Bobby Jones Expwy.
Martinez, GA 30907
800-374-4432
www.frigidaire.com
Manufactures a full line of outdoor grills, including models with infrared burners.

Gaco Western
P.O. Box 88698
Seattle, WA 98138
866-422-6489
www.gaco.com
Manufactures a high-quality acrylic polymer waterproof surface protection for plywood or plank decks.

Green Mountain Soapstone
680 East Hubbardton Rd.
Castleton, VT 05735
802-468-5636
www.greenmountainsoapstone.com
Produces soapstone sinks and countertops.

Hadco Lighting
100 Craftway
Littlestown, PA 17340

800-331-4185
www.hadco.com
Offers a variety of outdoor lighting designed for decks, including post, step, path, and area lights.

Heat & Glo
20802 Kensington Blvd.
Lakeville, MN 55044
888-427-3973
www.heatnglo.com
Offers a complete line of gas, wood, and electric fireplaces.

Highpoint Deck Lighting
P.O. Box 428
Black Hawk, CO 80422
888-582-5850
www.hpdlighting.com
Produces a full line of outdoor lighting, including railing lights, step lights, hanging lanterns, and wall sconces.

IntelliCool
1126 Commerce Dr.
Richardson, TX 75081
800-824-6567
www.intellicool.com
Manufactures outdoor climate- and environmental-control systems as well as a mosquito-repellant system.

KitchenAid
P.O. Box 218
St. Joseph, MI 49085
800-541-6390
www.kitchenaid.com
Manufactures a wide range of outdoor appliances.

Kohler
444 Highland Dr.
Kohler, WI 53044
800-456-4537
www.kohler.com
Manufactures sinks and faucets.

Landscape Perceptions
130 Ryerson Ave., Ste. 301
Wayne, NJ 07470
973-694-6545
www.landper.com
Designs and builds outdoor kitchens.

Laneventure
P.O. Box 849

Conover, NC 28613
800-235-3558
www.laneventure.com
Offers a variety of outdoor furniture and accessories.

Lasertron, Inc.
14251 NW 4th St.
Sunrise, FL 33325
954-846-8600
www.lasertrondirect.com
Manufactures stainless-steel outdoor kitchen cabinets with a wood look.

Living Elements
2046 Country Rd. 115
Burnet, TX 78611
512-756-0702
www.livingelements.com
Manufactures mesquite countertops and hand-cast copper and brass sinks.

Lloyd/Flanders, Inc.
3010 10th St.
Menominee, MI 49858
800-526-9894
www.lloydflanders.com
Produces loom and vinyl wicker outdoor furniture.

Lynx Professional Grills
6023 East Bandini Blvd.
Commerce, CA 90040
888-879-2322
www.lynxprofessionalgrills.com
Manufactures stainless-steel grills, side burners, refrigerators, warming drawers, ice machines, and more for the outdoors.

Marvel Industries
P.O. Box 997
Richmond, IN 47375
800-428-6644
www.marvelindustries.com
Manufactures outdoor appliances including refrigerators, ice machines, wine coolers, and beer dispensers.

McHale Landscape Design, Inc.
6212 Leapley Rd.
Upper Marlboro, MD 20772
301-599-8300
www.mchalelandscape.com
Designs and builds outdoor kitchens in addition to being a full-service landscape design company.

Moen
25300 Al Moen Dr.
North Olmsted, OH 44070
800-289-6636
www.moen.com
Manufactures sinks and faucets.

Mosquito Curtains Inc.
5725 Roberts Dr.
Atlanta, GA 30338
866-622-0916
www.mosquitocurtains.com
Offers custom-made curtains made of mosquito netting.

NanaWall Systems, Inc.
707 Redwood Hwy.
Mill Valley, CA 94941
800-873-5673
www.nanawall.com
Manufactures folding wall systems of easy-to-open glass panels.

Native Trails
4173 Santa Fe Rd., Ste. A
San Luis Obispo, CA 93401
800-786-0862
www.nativetrails.net
Manufactures handcrafted copper sinks, tubs, vanities, and accessories.

Nautilus Cabinetry
4120 Enterprise Ave., Ste. 111
Naples, FL 34104
800-975-2805
www.nautiluscabinetry.com
Manufactures outdoor cabinetry constructed of marine polymer, teak, and cypress. Also offers a variety of outdoor refrigerators, grills, and range hoods.

Outdoor Kitchen Cabinets & More
1823 Lakewood Ranch Blvd.
Bradenton, FL 34211
941-744-5000
www.outdoorkitchencabinetsandmore.com
Offers polymer cabinets, countertops, appliances and grills.

The Outdoor Kitchen Store
3925 West Kennedy Blvd.
Tampa, FL 33609
813-875-3447
www.outdoorkitchenstore.com

Offers guidance in outdoor kitchen planning, and sells grills, smokers, TVs, refrigerators, and accessories for the outdoors.

Owens Corning Cultured Stone
One Owens Corning Pkwy.
Toledo, OH 43659
800-255-1727
www.culturedstone.com
Manufactures a variety of cultured stone styles for outdoor use.

Progress Lighting
P.O. Box 5704
Spartanburg, SC 29304-5704
864-599-6000
www.progresslighting.com
Produces a variety of outdoor lighting fixtures, including wall lanterns, deck lights, and landscape lights.

ShadeScapes USA
39300 Back River Rd.
Paonia, CO 81428
866-997-4233
www.shadescapesusa.com
Manufactures side- and center-post shade umbrellas.

ShadeTree
6317 Busch Blvd.
Columbus, OH 43229
800-894-3801
www.shadetreecanopies.com
Manufactures retractable canopy systems that are water repellant and help block UV rays.

Solaire/Rasmussen Iron Works, Inc.
12028 East Philadelphia St.
Whittier, CA 90601
562-696-8718
www.rasmussen.biz
Manufactures stainless-steel infrared grills.

Sonoma Cast Stone
133A Copeland St.
Petaluma, CA 94952
877-283-2400
www.sonomastone.com
Produces concrete sinks, countertops, and surrounds.

Stecks Nursery and Landscaping
100 Putnam Park Rd.
Bethel, CT 06801

800-800-9732
www.atstecks.com
Designs and builds decks, patios, and outdoor kitchens.

Summer Classics
7000 Hwy. 25
Montevallo, AL 35115
205-987-3100
www.summerclassics.com
Designs and manufactures fine garden furniture, umbrellas, and decorative cushions.

SunBriteTV
5069 Maureen Ln., Unit A
Moorpark, CA 93021
866-357-8688
www.sunbritetv.com
Manufactures all-weather outdoor LCD televisions.

SunPorch Structures Inc.
495 Post Rd. East
Westport, CT 06880
203-454-0040
www.sunporch.com
Manufactures ready-to-assemble sunroom kits.

Syndecrete
2908 Colorado Ave.
Santa Monica, CA 90404
310-829-9704
www.syndecrete.com
Manufactures and designs solid-surface tiles, sinks, countertops, and tabletops for the outdoors.

Texas Pit Crafters
31909 Decker Industrial Dr.
Pinehurst, TX 77362
877-697-7487
www.texaspitcrafters.com
Manufactures grills, smokers, and outdoor kitchens.

TIC Corporation
15224 East Stafford St.
City of Industry, CA 91744-4418
www.ticcorp.com
626-968-0211
Designs, produces, distributes, and installs exterior-grade audio systems.

TimberTech
894 Prairie Ave.

Wilmington, OH 45177
800-307-7780
www.timbertech.com
Manufactures composite decking and railing systems, fascia boards, and specialty trim.

Traeger Pellet Grills
990 North First St.
Silverton, OR 97381
800-872-3437
www.traegergrills.com
Designs and manufactures wood pellet grills.

Trex Company, Inc.
160 Exeter Dr.
Winchester, VA 22603
800-289-8739
www.trex.com
Manufactures composite decking and railing products.

U-Line Corporation
P.O. Box 245040
Milwaukee, WI 53224-9540
414-354-0300
www.u-line.com
Manufactures a full line of refrigeration appliances for outdoor use, including refrigerators, ice makers, and freezers.

Viking
111 Front St.
Greenwood, MS 38930
662-455-1200
www.vikingrange.com
Manufactures gas grills, range hoods, stainless-steel cabinets, and other products for outdoor living.

Weber-Stephen Products Co.
200 East Daniels Rd.
Palatine, IL 60067-6266
800-446-1071
www.weber.com
Manufactures charcoal and gas grills, grilling accessories, and other outdoor products.

Wer/Ever Outdoor Products, Inc.
3900 South 50th St.
Tampa, FL 33619
888-324-3837
www.werever.com
Manufactures weatherproof outdoor cabinets from solid marine-grade polymer.

GLOSSARY

Backer board   A ready-made panel made with nylon mesh and a cement or gypsum core that is used as a substrate for ceramic-tile installations or other facings.

Balusters   The vertical pieces that fill the spaces between rails and posts to create a guardrail.

Balustrade   A guardrail, often used around the perimeter of a deck or raised patio, consisting of balusters, posts, and top and bottom rails.

Brad   A thin nail with a small, barrel-shaped head.

British thermal unit (Btu)   The amount of energy needed to raise the temperature of 1 pound of water by 1 degree Fahrenheit. It's used to describe how much energy a grill can produce from the gas it burns.

Building codes   Municipal rules regulating safe building practices and procedures. Generally, the codes encompass structural, electrical, plumbing, and mechanical remodeling and new construction.

Building permit   An authorization to build or renovate according to plans approved by the local building department. Generally, any job that includes a foundation or that involves structural work requires a permit.

Chamfer   A flat surface made by planing the edge or corner of a piece of wood.

Clad   To sheathe or cover with a metal.

Clearance   The amount of recommended space between two fixtures, such as between a grill and wall.

Cleat   A piece of wood or metal that is fastened to a structural member to support or provide a point of attachment for another member or fixture.

Composite   Building materials that are made by combining wood waste or fiber with plastics.

Concrete   A strong building material made by mixing cement, sand, gravel or crushed stone, and water.

Dry well   A hole in the ground filled with stones or gravel used to receive and disburse drainage water.

Elevation drawing   An architectural drawing of a structure seen from the side, rear, or front view.

Facing   A surface material used on the exterior of grill counters and other structures.

Fire pit   A built-in masonry well used to contain a fire. Some portable metal hearths are also called fire pits.

Floor plan   A two-dimensional scale drawing that shows the top-down view of a room (or rooms), the arrangement of fixtures, and its dimensions.

Footing   A concrete pad, usually at the frost line, that supports posts, piers, or stairs.

Footprint   The area on a surface covered by something.

Frost heave   Upheaval of the ground resulting from the alternate freezing and thawing of water in soil.

Frost line   The maximum depth at which soil freezes in a given locale. Footings generally must sit below the frost line in colder climates.

Gable   A triangular part or structure, especially the triangular end of a double-sloping roof.

Grade   The finished level of the ground surrounding a landscaping or construction project. Also, the planned level of the ground around a project that is in progress.

Gray water   Household wastewater (from a sink, for example) that does not contain serious contaminants.

Grommet   A small ring used to reinforce an eyelet.

Ground-fault circuit interrupter (GFCI)   A device that monitors the loss of current in an electrical circuit. If an interruption occurs, the GFCI quickly shuts off current to that circuit.

Guardrail   An assembly of posts, balusters (or some other material), and rails that is usually installed around the perimeter of a deck for safety.

Handrail   A narrow railing at stairs that is designed to be grasped by the hand for support.

Heartwood   The older, nonliving inner core of a tree that may have decay- and insect-resistant properties.

High definition polyethylene (HDPE)   A petroleum-based dense plastic, often recycled from milk jugs and plastic bags, used to make composite lumber.

Infrared   Radiation produced by certain grill burners that is situated outside the visible spectrum at its red end. The infrared burner focuses the flame of a standard gas burner onto a ceramic tile or stainless-steel burner that has thousands of microscopic holes in it. This converts the heat of the flame into infrared energy, creating a uniform heat that is much higher and more direct than a standard grill can produce.

Inlay   A decorative item set into a surface (of a countertop, for example). Also, to adorn with insertions.

Island   A unit consisting of base cabinets and countertop that stands independent from walls and has access from all four sides. Also called a grill counter.

Joist   A structural member commonly placed perpendicularly across beams to support deck boards.

Lath   A building material used as a base for stucco.

Lattice   An open framework made of wood, metal, or plastic strips—usually preassembled and typically in a crisscross pattern—that's used to build trellises, windscreens, and skirting.

LED lighting   Long-lasting lighting that conserves electricity. LED stands for light-emitting diode.

Lee   The side or area that is sheltered from the wind.

Low-voltage lighting   Easy-to-install outdoor lighting fixtures that are powered by low-voltage direct current.

Manufactured stone   A material made from concrete and color pigments that looks very similar to natural stone but weighs less.

Masonry   A structure made of concrete block, brick, stone, or poured concrete.

Mortar   A compound of cement, sand, water, and sometimes lime. It is usually used to provide a stable base for stone or ceramic tile.

Onlay   Something laid or applied over something else, as to add relief to a surface.

Plan drawing   A drawing that shows an overhead view of the outdoor kitchen and specifies dimensions, along with the locations and sizes of components.

Polymer   A plastic-like material, produced with chemical compounds, that's used to create coatings, sheet goods, and many other useful products.

Pressure-treated (PT) lumber   Wood that has had preservative forced into it under pressure to make it decay- and insect-resistant.

PVC   A common thermoplastic resin, frequently called vinyl, used in a variety of building products.

Rabbet   A recess cut along the edge of a piece of wood so it can receive another piece, or the joint formed by fitting together rabbeted boards. Also, to join the edges in a rabbet joint, or to cut in a rabbet.

Rail   A horizontal member that runs between two vertical supports, such as the rails between posts of a deck.

Range hood   A ventilator set above a grill, cooktop, or range. Also called a vent hood or an exhaust hood.

Rotisserie   A cooking device equipped with a slowly rotating spit on which meat or other food is roasted.

Scale   The relationship of a structure's size to people, nearby objects, and the surrounding space. Also, the relationship of elements of a structure to the whole.

Setback   The legally required distance of a structure or some other feature from the property line.

Sheathing   Panels or boards applied to a building's framework and upon which siding or roofing is installed.

Side burner   A burner that fits on the side of a grill and is often used to boil water, heat sauces, or stir-fry vegetables.

Site plan   A drawing that maps out a house and yard. Also called a base plan.

Smoker   A cooking unit that slowly smokes meat at a low temperature to produce tender pieces of meat.

Stile   One of the vertical members in a frame into which the secondary members are fitted.

Stucco   A surface finish, often applied by hand, that consists of multiple layers of mortar.

Synthetic decking   Any engineered decking material made from plastics or composites.

Tilt-out   A shallow tray in front of the sink that pivots out for storing sponges, brushes, soap, and so forth.

Ultraviolet (UV) light   The range of invisible radiation wavelengths, just beyond violet in the visible spectrum, that can be particularly damaging to outdoor wood structures.

Vinyl   A tough, flexible plastic that is used especially for flooring, siding, decking, and railing. Also called PVC.

Windbreak   A shelter from the wind. A fence or a growth of trees or shrubs can serve as a windbreak.

Work triangle   The area bounded by the lines that connect the sink, range, and refrigerator. In theory, the sum of the line lengths should not exceed 26 feet.

INDEX

PHOTO CREDITS

page 1: Sudi Scull **page 3:** courtesy of Fogazzo Wood Fired Ovens and Barbecues **page 5:** courtesy of Fire Stone Home Products **page 6:** Home & Garden Editorial Services **page 7:** *top* courtesy of Viking; *bottom* Lars Dalsgaard **pages 8-9:** Pete Bleyer, design: Peter Schechter **page 10:** *top* courtesy of U-Line Corporation; *bottom* courtesy of Native Trails **page 11:** *top* courtesy of Syndecrete; *bottom* courtesy of Eldorado Stone **pages 12-13:** courtesy of KitchenAid **pages 14-16:** Crandall & Crandall **page 17:** courtesy of McHale Landscape Design, Inc., photography by Erin Brooke Bogan **pages 18-19:** courtesy of McHale Landscape Design, Inc., photography by Erin Brooke Bogan **pages 20-21:** Crandall & Crandall **page 22:** courtesy of Owens Corning Cultured Stone **page 23:** Crandall & Crandall **page 24:** courtesy of KitchenAid **pages 25-27:** Lars Dalsgaard **pages 28-29:** Brian Vanden Brink **page 30:** courtesy of KitchenAid **page 31:** courtesy of Western Red Cedar Lumber Association **page 32:** courtesy of McHale Landscape Design, Inc., photography by Erin Brooke Bogan **page 33:** courtesy of Fogazzo Wood Fired Ovens and Barbecues **page 34:** *top* courtesy of McHale Landscape Design, Inc., photography by Erin Brooke Bogan; *middle* courtesy of Outdoor Kitchen Cabinets & More; *bottom* courtesy of Fogazzo Wood Fired Ovens and Barbecues **page 35:** *top* courtesy of Nautilus Cabinetry; *bottom* courtesy of Country Casual **pages 36-37:** *top* courtesy of Anderson Corporation; *bottom* Mark Samu **pages 38-39:** courtesy of NanaWall Systems, Inc. **page 41:** courtesy of NanaWall Systems, Inc. **page 42:** Home & Garden Editorial Services **pages 44-45:** courtesy of Landscape Perceptions, design: Lenny DiTomaso **pages 46-47:** courtesy of Outdoor Kitchen Cabinets & More **pages 48-49:** courtesy of Fogazzo Wood Fired Ovens and Barbecues **pages 50-51:** *top left & bottom* courtesy of McHale Landscape Design, Inc., photography by Erin Brooke Bogan; *top right* Crandall & Crandall **pages 52-53:** courtesy of Trex Company, Inc. **pages 54-55:** *top* Crandall & Crandall; *bottom* courtesy of Stecks Nursery and Landscaping **pages 56-57:** *top* courtesy of CableRail/Feeney Architectural Products; *bottom* Home & Garden Editorial Services **page 58:** courtesy of TimberTech **page 59:** *top & bottom* courtesy of Trex Company, Inc.; *middle* courtesy of EverGrain Composite Decking **page 60:** courtesy of AridDek **page 61:** courtesy of Gaco Western **pages 62-63:** Crandall & Crandall **pages 64-65:** Zach DeSart **pages 66-67:** *left* courtesy of NanaWall Systems, Inc.; *right* courtesy of McHale Landscape Design, Inc., photography by Erin Brooke Bogan **page 68:** *top* Brian Vanden Brink; *bottom* courtesy of McHale Landscape Design, Inc., photography by Erin Brooke Bogan **page 69:** courtesy of McHale Landscape Design, Inc., photography by Erin Brooke Bogan **pages 70-71:** Mark Lohman **page 72:** David Cro **page 73:** *top &*

bottom right Crandall & Crandall; *bottom left* David Cro **pages 74-77:** Lars Dalsgaard **page 78:** courtesy of ShadeScapes USA **page 79:** *top* courtesy of ShadeScapes USA; *bottom left* Brian Vanden Brink; *bottom right* courtesy of ShadeScapes USA **page 80:** *top* courtesy of ShadeTree; *bottom* courtesy of Coolaroo **page 81:** *top* courtesy of Coolaroo; *bottom* courtesy of Country Casual **page 82:** Crandall & Crandall **page 83:** courtesy of McHale Landscape Design, Inc., photography by Erin Brooke Bogan **page 84:** courtesy of McHale Landscape Design, Inc., photography by Erin Brooke Bogan **page 85:** courtesy of SunPorch Structures Inc. **page 86:** Brian Vanden Brink **page 87:** Lars Dalsgaard **page 88:** *top* courtesy of IntelliCool; *bottom* courtesy of Owens Corning Cultured Stone **page 89:** *left* courtesy of IntelliCool; *right* courtesy of Blue Rhino Corporation **pages 90-91:** courtesy of Hadco Lighting **page 93:** *top* courtesy of Outdoor Kitchen Cabinets & More; *bottom* courtesy of Fire Magic **page 94:** *top* courtesy of Cal Spas; *bottom* courtesy of McHale Landscape Design, Inc., photography by Erin Brooke Bogan **page 97:** courtesy of CableRail/Feeney Architectural Products **page 98:** courtesy of Hadco Lighting **page 99:** *top left & top middle* courtesy of Highpoint Deck Lighting; *top right* courtesy of Progress Lighting; *bottom* courtesy of Hadco Lighting **page 100:** courtesy of Cal Spas **page 101:** *top* courtesy of Cal Spas; *bottom* courtesy of Heat & Glo **pages 102-103:** courtesy of Chicago Specialty Gardens **pages 104-105:** courtesy of Viking **page 106:** courtesy of KitchenAid **page 107:** Pete Blyer **page 108:** courtesy of Viking **page 109:** courtesy of Fire Magic **page 110:** *top* © 2007 Weber-Stephen Products Co.; *bottom* courtesy of Char-Broil **page 111:** courtesy of KitchenAid **page 112:** © 2006 Weber-Stephen Products Co. **page 113:** *top* courtesy of Dacor; *bottom* courtesy of Traeger Pellet Grills **page 114:** *top left, bottom left, & top right* courtesy of Fire Magic; *middle right* courtesy of Viking; *bottom right* courtesy of Fire Magic **page 115:** *top left & middle left* courtesy of Fire Magic; *bottom left, top right, & bottom right* courtesy of Viking **page 116:** courtesy of Char-Broil **page 117:** courtesy of Fogazzo Wood Fired Ovens and Barbecues **page 118:** Pete Bleyer, design: Peter Schechter **page 119:** *top left & bottom right* courtesy of Viking; *bottom left* courtesy of Marvel Industries **pages 120-121:** Pete Bleyer, design: Peter Schechter **page 122:** courtesy of Green Mountain Soapstone **page 123:** courtesy of Nautilus Cabinetry **page 124:** Sudi Scull **page 125:** courtesy of Lasertron, Inc. **page 126:** courtesy of Fogazzo Wood Fired Ovens and Barbecues **page 127:** *top* courtesy of Advanced Concrete Enhancement; *bottom* Crandall & Crandall **page 129:** *top* courtesy of Wer/Ever Outdoor Products, Inc.; *bottom* courtesy of Classic Garden Design **pages 130-131:** courtesy of Stecks Nursery and Landscaping **page**

132: courtesy of Classic Garden Design **page 133:** *top left* courtesy of Kohler; *top right* courtesy of Native Trails; *bottom* courtesy of Kohler **page 134:** courtesy of Living Elements **page 135:** *top & middle* courtesy of Kohler; *bottom* courtesy of Green Mountain Soapstone **pages 136-138:** courtesy of Moen **page 139:** *top* courtesy of Kohler; *bottom* Mark Lohman **page 140:** *top* courtesy of Cal Spas; *bottom left* courtesy of Viking; *bottom right* courtesy of Atlantis Cabinetry **page 141:** courtesy of Country Casual **pages 142-143:** Pete Bleyer, design: Peter Schechter **pages 144-145:** courtesy of Fogazzo Wood Fired Ovens and Barbecues **page 146:** *top* Mark Samu; *bottom* courtesy of Atlantis Cabinetry **page 148:** *top* courtesy of Classic Garden Design; *bottom* courtesy of Texas Pit Crafters **pages 150-152:** courtesy of Cal Spas **page 153:** *top* courtesy of Cal Spas; *bottom* courtesy of Barbeques Galore **page 154:** *top* courtesy of Fire Magic; *middle* courtesy of Marvel Industries; *bottom* courtesy of Viking **page 155:** courtesy of Viking **page 156:** courtesy of Danver **page 157:** *top* courtesy of Atlantis Cabinetry; *middle* courtesy of Lasertron, Inc.; *bottom* courtesy of Classic Home Elements **pages 158-159:** courtesy of Atlantis Cabinetry **page 160:** *top* courtesy of Classic Home Elements; *middle & bottom right* courtesy of Atlantis Cabinetry; *bottom left* courtesy of Wer/Ever Outdoor Products, Inc. **page 161:** *top* courtesy of Wer/Ever Outdoor Products, Inc.; *middle & bottom right* courtesy of Nautilus Cabinetry; *bottom left* courtesy of Atlantis Cabinetry **page 162:** courtesy of Country Casual **page 163:** courtesy of Cal Spas **pages 164-165:** courtesy of Chicago Specialty Gardens **page 166:** Crandall & Crandall **page 167:** *top & bottom right* courtesy of Atlantis Cabinetry; *bottom left* courtesy of Laneventure **pages 168-169:** courtesy of Chicago Specialty Gardens **page 170:** courtesy of Country Casual **page 171:** *top* courtesy of Summer Classics; *bottom left* courtesy of Laneventure; *bottom right* courtesy of Lloyd/Flanders Inc. **page 172:** courtesy of Lloyd/Flanders Inc. **page 173:** *left & top right* courtesy of Laneventure; *bottom right* courtesy of Lloyd/Flanders Inc. **pages 174-177:** Lars Dalsgaard **pages 178-179:** courtesy of Conrad Imports, Inc. **page 180:** *top left & right* courtesy of SunBriteTV; *bottom* courtesy of TIC Corporation **page 181:** Brian Vanden Brink **page 182:** courtesy of Conrad Imports, Inc. **page 183:** *top* courtesy of Coolaroo; *bottom* courtesy of Laneventure **pages 184-185:** Home & Garden Editorial Services **page 187:** *top* courtesy of Chicago Specialty Gardens; *bottom* courtesy of Hadco Lighting **pages 188-189:** Pete Bleyer, design: Peter Schechter **pages 190-195:** Home & Garden Editorial Services **pages 196-199:** Pete Bleyer **page 201:** Dry-B-Lo **pages 202-205:** Lars Dalsgaard **pages 206-207:** courtesy of APA – The Engineered Wood Association **pages 208-211:** Lars Dalsgaard **page 223:** Sudi Scull

Have a home improvement, decorating, or gardening project? Look for these and other fine **Creative Homeowner books** wherever books are sold.

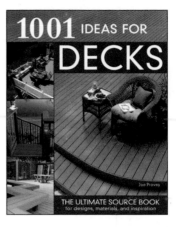

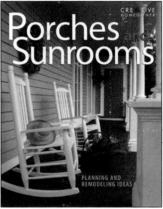
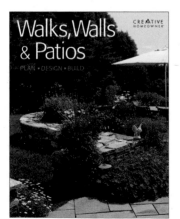